From Kefir, With Love.

The **Complete Guide** to
Making Kefir and
Healing Your Gut — Naturally

By Whitney Wilson

From Kefir, With Love by Whitney Wilson

www.KefirLove.com

© 2018 Whitney Wilson

All rights reserved. No portion of this book may be reproduced in any form without permission from the publisher, except as permitted by U.S. copyright law. For permissions contact:

info@kefirlove.com

ISBN: 9781980441540

Table of Contents

AUTHOR'S NOTE..1

PART ONE: WHY SHOULD I CARE ABOUT KEFIR?

CHAPTER ONE: HOW I FELT..9
CHAPTER TWO: ENTER, KEFIR..16
CHAPTER THREE: A NEW PERSPECTIVE.......................................22
CHAPTER FOUR: BEHIND YOUR BELLY BUTTON......................30
CHAPTER FIVE: MICROBIOME & DYSBIOSIS...............................36
CHAPTER SIX: PROBIOTICS & PREBIOTICS.................................46
CHAPTER SEVEN: DIGESTION..54
CHAPTER EIGHT: EVERYTHING IS CONNECTED......................66
CHAPTER NINE: SANITIZATION NATION....................................78

PART 2: THIS IS KEFIR

CHAPTER TEN: THE KEFIR STORY...92
CHAPTER ELEVEN: WHAT IS KEFIR?..100
CHAPTER TWELVE: KEFIR GRAINS 101..108
CHAPTER THIRTEEN: HOW TO MAKE KEFIR.............................116
CHAPTER FOURTEEN: THE ART OF PERFECT KEFIR...............122
CHAPTER FIFTEEN: DIFFERENT MILK TYPES............................132
CHAPTER SIXTEEN: WATER KEFIR...138
CHAPTER SEVENTEEN: THE BENEFITS OF KEFIR....................146
CHAPTER EIGHTEEN: THE KEFIR MYSTIQUE............................160
CHAPTER NINETEEN: THE APPETITE FOR THINGS NATURAL.....168
CHAPTER TWENTY: SO WHAT?..176

PART 3: RECIPES & RESOURCES

CHAPTER TWENTY-ONE: QUICK REFFERENCE GUIDE.............184
CHAPTER TWENTY-TWO: SMOOTHIE RECIPES.........................196
CHAPTER TWENTY-THREE: SECOND FERMENTS.....................200
CHAPTER TWENTY-FOUR: WATER KEFIR RECIPES..................204
CHAPTER TWENTY-FIVE: HOW TO MAKE KEFIR CHEESE.....206
CHAPTER TWENTY-SIX: KEFIR SKIN CARE..................................210

ABOUT THE AUTHOR..214
REFERENCES..218

About Me

My name is Whitney.

When I was facing my health demons I accidentally stumbled upon Kefir. What started with a few simple web searches eventually turned into thousands of hours, and many years, of dedicated research into what probiotics really mean to the human body and how our gut health governs our lives. I was amazed to discover that so much amazing research was essentially tucked away in academia, hidden from the rest of the world.

I made it my personal mission to bring all this hidden information into the light, or at least as much as I could!

Kefir is no gimmick. It's a miracle. It changed my life.

I'm sure it can help you, too!

- Whit

Author's Note

How Do You Feel?

Whoever you are, I'd like you to know one thing: I wrote this book because I want to help you feel better.

As you'll soon read, I know what it's like to feel terrible. I know what it feels like to be unhealthy. I know the feeling of having my entire body ache while lying on the bathroom floor. I know what it's like to wake up, roll out of bed, and nearly fall to the ground because I was too weak. I know what it's like to look back at an earlier, healthier, stronger version of myself and wonder what happened. I've felt the sting of looking into the mirror and, seeing that health and vitality had left my body, wonder how it all happened. If this shared misery is any consolation to you, please take heart, you have a friend.

And, while I freely admit that I don't have all the answers—or the magic bullet for perfect health—I will say that what I have found is powerful and transformational enough to motivate me to dedicate thousands of hours of my life to it. I can't promise to take away all your ailments, but I can offer help, and with it, hope.

Pain, discomfort, and disease are very personal things. We don't talk about them much to others, except for possibly members of our family or close friends. For some reason, it seems instinctual to deal with our health elements in secret. Perhaps it's cultural, maybe it's a social taboo to discuss such things as our aches and pains in public. I mean, we want to be seen as healthy, strong, and vibrant, right? Like, who goes around on social media and talks about how terrible they feel all the time, or that they're mad or ashamed they're not as healthy as they want to be? Last time I checked, my Facebook feed isn't exactly filled with phrases such as "Hey, I have more autoimmune diseases than you can count!", "You should see Johnny's colon polyps, they're the biggest in his class!", or "My belly bloated so big after that brownie, you'd think I was the blueberry chick from that movie with the Oompa Loompas!"

No, I dare say, we tend to keep those things rather hush-hush.

So, if that's you—if you're suffering in secret—please know that you're probably part of a very large, relatively silent, majority. I have a news flash for you: all of our shit stinks, and if we weren't all too embarrassed to talk about it, maybe it'd stink a little less (more on that later).

My point is this: I know it can be awkward to talk about the things that hurt us. It isn't fun thinking about the diseases we have or the pains we feel. But, as you enter this book with an eye to possibly find some healing information tucked inside these chapters, I ask you to do so with a bit of vulnerability. Open yourself up to your pain, discomfort, and sickness. Don't embrace it, but acknowledge it. Recognize it for what it is, and let's get started seeing what we can do about it. If you can't trust anyone else in the world in talking about, or working though, your ailments, then at the very least know that I am here, in written form, to offer whatever helping hand I can. As

I mentioned before, I don't have the magic bullet, but I'm human—just like you. I'm someone else out there who got sicker than I ever thought I would be and I came out on the other side healthy, happy, and wiser for the journey.

Will you do something for me that will probably feel a bit silly? I'm going to test your commitment to being vulnerable here. Will you take your hand and place it on your belly? I know, it's weird. But, no matter where you are right now, I promise no one around you is going to care. Take your right hand now, and just place it on your stomach.

I'll wait....

Ok, now leave it there for a bit. Take a deep breath. I want you to do something that 90% of Americans have NEVER done—think about your gut. Seriously, take 60 seconds and consider what's going on inside there, just a few inches from the palm of your hand right now. What do you feel? Does it feel full? Empty? Bloated? Tight? Bubbly? Painful? Calm? Consider for just a moment what's going on in there right now.

Your stomach is just finishing up processing the food you just ate. The acids have broken it down and it is beginning to make its way into your intestinal tract, where it will continue to be broken down and its nutrients (or lack thereof) will be absorbed into your body to keep you alive. Did you know there are bacteria in there? Billions and trillions of them? Living, tiny little organisms doing your dirty work of breaking down your food and helping you get ready to shit. What pals! More than just food, did you know your gut is tied to your brain? To your mood? To your overall feeling of wellbeing? In fact, it could be argued that, aside from your beating heart and breathing lungs, the activity in your gut is the single most important process that keeps you alive, and, more specifically, feeling healthy. If you're like most people, you've probably never given it a second thought, except for that raised eyebrow after a particularly stinky fart.

Ok, you can take your hand off now. Thanks for indulging with me on that one. The reason for that exercise? I want you to start to think about your gut. I want you to understand the healing potential it has, and that many of the ailments, diseases, and pains you feel, even if they don't seem gut related, can be healed by giving your gut a little TLC.

If you remember nothing else from this little exercise, remember this:

Your Gut Has Everything to Do with How You Feel.

If you can hang on to that idea, and stick with me as I explain how kefir fits into all of this, I think you're going to start to feel—really feel—better, in a genuine and substantial way.

Part One

Why Should I Care About Kefir?

Chapter One

How I Felt

"It is loss that teaches us about the worth of things."
-Unknown

People Just Want to Feel Healthy

Health struggles are universal. They are the touchstone of humanity—our frailty of being mortal. No two people experience the myriad of life's health problems in exactly the same way. But, everyone is looking for something better than their current hand offers them. When you find yourself in poor health, whether you caused it or not, you're probably willing to do whatever it takes to feel better. We want to dip into the fountain of youth and remain unscathed from illness and disease. We want to really experience a body that is free from pain, inflammation, and the burden of disease.

Here's the thing about trying to be healthy: people aren't willing to change unless they can feel a real and tangible benefit. I'm not usually willing to go through the discomfort of change unless I believe something will actually be different at the end of the change process. For example, when you experience a problem with your health, you normally go to the doctor, right? When you visit your doctor for treatment, you are usually provided with a report of your health. This may include stats on things like blood pressure and heart rate, along with other basic vital signs. But many of those "health metrics" are just obscure numbers. You and I are not likely to change our behavior just to see a few digits drop on some computerized spreadsheet. However, we are far more motivated to change if we feel something different. We take risks and put in effort when we see the possibility of a tangible, positive outcome.

The reason people put in the effort to lose weight is because they want to feel better with less body fat to carry around and feel more confident in their skin. The reason people exercise is because their body feels more energy with which to tackle their tasks of the day. The reason people practice meditation is because their mind feels clearer afterward.

Human motivation has always been closely associated with the ability to see and feel the reasons why.

In short, we all want to feel better today than we did yesterday. Nobody really believes that things can change overnight, but if we can notice a difference—an improvement from day to day—that is what provides hope for a better life than you had yesterday.

If I look at the people that surround my life—my family & friends—I'm sad to see that many of them don't live with the health they want. This was a surprise because I consider most of my family and friends to be healthy, active people. I doubt there are more than a few who would say they are completely satisfied with their current health. Most of them have to live with the effects of painful autoimmune diseases, diabetes, depression, stress, sleep issues, and much more. Take a moment to think about that yourself. Think about your own friends and family. Of all the people you know, how many of them to you think are truly, fully content with their current health? I would venture to guess it's a very small number.

Of course, this isn't just an issue for the people you and I know personally. This is a national problem, too. According to the Centers for Disease Control and Prevention (CDC), one out of every two US adults has a chronic disease[1]. That's half the adult population… that's 117 MILLION Americans with heart disease, diabetes, obesity, cancer or other chronic disease. These are the kinds of conditions that cannot be prevented by vaccines and that cannot be cured with medication. And, nearly all of these conditions are the result of a lifetime of choices. Here are some more facts that show just how severe the national state of our health is:

- 1 out of 4 (25%) adults have TWO chronic diseases
- 3 out of 4 (75%) in the 65+ age group have two chronic diseases
- Chronic diseases are responsible for 7 out of 10 deaths each year
- Chronic diseases account for 86% of our national healthcare costs

There's a national conversation going on right now about healthcare and how it should work. Fixing health problems is multi-faceted and cannot be addressed with just one solution, however. But, I guarantee you one thing: most people don't know how to feel better, even when the possibility of feeling better is out there. Many people are in a health crisis and don't know how to get out of it. The problem is that mainstream "health" advice has never helped me, and I'm sure it's not helping you. Slashing calories, joining up with fad diets, "fitness" trends and expensive supplements or training plans never lead to lasting change. More importantly, they don't help you feel great.

Band-Aids for your health transformation has never led to you feeling the way you truly desire.

How I Felt... Before

27 years old is not the age I ever expected to have a health crisis.

When I say that sickness was a new experience for me, I totally mean it. I've been blessed to have these great Swiss genetics that are actually quite remarkable. Everybody in my paternal blood line is pretty much unscathed by cancer or other major disease. Likewise, I have never had anything more serious than a sinus infection. Before I met my husband, I had only set foot in a hospital a few times... and never for myself. My Dad is healthy, and my grandparents are even healthier. In fact, my grandpa was picking dozens of tomatoes from his very own garden until the day he died. To put it simply, I was very lucky.

Fast forward to July 2016. My husband and I planned our first pregnancy. I knew I was pregnant even before I even had a chance to pee on a stick. It was obvious to me that something was different. I didn't feel "normal." It started with feeling dizzy when I stood up, especially in the mornings. Within a few days I had a constant, nauseated tummy-churning feeling, but nothing too serious... yet. If you don't know anything about pregnancy nausea, this is not when most ladies start to get nauseous. The nausea turned into vomiting, and it seemed to escalate out of control almost overnight. I was only about five weeks into the pregnancy when it got completely out of control. I will never forget the first night things really got bad. I started throwing up when my husband went to bed and was dry heaving every hour till morning. There was no break to take a sip of anything. I got to the point where the pain of it all was so bad that the thought of "my baby is in danger" kept flickering in my mind. The next morning, my husband took me to the hospital where was treated with IV treatment, which helped, for the moment.

After the hospital, though, I had a difficult time with doctors taking me seriously about the condition of my nausea. They refused to talk about treatment options until I had lost 10% of my weight, at which point they would have diagnosed me with Hyperemesis Gravadium (extreme pregnancy nausea). It's at that same point, however, that babies actually are at risk and so is the mother's health. Long-lasting complications from extreme dehydration and nutritional deprivation can have intense consequences. If I was going to feel better, I had to do my own research. I found and asked for specific prescriptions to try. Luckily, I found a lovely little pill that helped. It didn't cure me by any means, but it curbed the "I'm going to die" feeling. My husband and I joke now that that little pill is a sacred substance in our household—it was a saving grace. I was one of the lucky ones with extreme nausea who found something that worked.

But life wasn't all flowers and sunshine after I got help. I was still really sick—like sick enough that my friends and family didn't see me for months kind of sick. I could still only sip apple juice and chew on ice and Cheerios for the first four months. I couldn't cook or clean my house. I couldn't be too close to people because their scent made me sick. Life was completely thrown upside down. What was once an active life became a miserable life. I often joke now that my passion for weight lifting was exchanged for toilet squats, and my yoga blocks were turned into barfing stools.

You might be thinking, "So, what? You threw up for 9 months." Well sure, I survived the vomiting, but it tore my body to shreds. It destroyed it. Nine months of depleted nutrition and months of being confined to a bed/couch can really do a lot of harm. Every ounce of muscle I had before—the muscle that could deadlift 200 pounds—was gone. My meticulously maintained and balanced diet, out the window. I was so weak I couldn't even hold my body up straight while standing. Literally. I was so weak that even three months after

I had my baby my husband still needed to help me get out of bed. I would roll over, and he would push me over the edge. We would laugh about it, and it became a kind of joke, but inside I was completely ashamed. I was achy and tired 100% of the time. Simple tasks, like holding my baby and throwing the ball for the dog, were hard—like discouragingly hard. I remember going to a field close our home by with my dog, Rue, about a month and a half postpartum. I threw the tennis ball and it went a measly 10 yards. I thought, "Wow, I used to throw the ball a lot farther than this."

It was very apparent that there was no "bouncing back" for me.

Turning Point

It came just by luck.

I had this beautiful, tiny baby that I adored. But she had a huge barfing problem! So, like many breastfeeding mothers before me, I cut all dairy out of my diet. The idea was that the lactose found in the dairy made its way into my breastmilk, causing reflux in my little one. All milk proteins: whey, casein, milkfat, etc.—gone. Now, I would never have done this if it weren't for my baby. To be clear, I am not recommending anybody cut an entire food group out unless advised by a professional. Thankfully for me, though, it helped! My baby began spitting up less and it was a huge solution to my laundry problem (baby barf just gets annoying, you know!).

But the real shocker came with how I felt!! I had never felt so transformed in such a short amount of time. It was incredible! Within two days I felt like a ton of bricks had been lifted out of my gut. The fog was lifted from my mind, and I had the energy to feel like a normal human being again. It was that shocking result that made me want to shout from the rooftops. For the first time in a year, I felt hope that I could feel well again.

Here's the thing though—I had no idea I was feeling that terrible. I knew I was tired; obviously I had just pushed a baby out of my vagina, but this change was so sudden and unexpected, it caught me off guard. It was like someone finally turned on the light in a dark room. Have you ever felt that before? Where something makes so much sense that you are shocked you didn't realize it before? When you're living with a foggy brain and a lack of mental sharpness, you don't recognize the severity of your situation.

When those lights turned on, though, I started looking at the rest of my health. It was like my mind had illuminated just enough to realize that dairy wasn't the only problem. I started asking the questions "How did I get here with my health?" "What else could be wrong with me?" "Why don't I feel normal yet?"

I knew that I felt better after cutting out dairy, but my intuition was telling me it was only the tip of the iceberg. I felt better, but I didn't feel right.

Something was still missing.

Chapter Two

Enter, Kefir

"Look for something, find something else, and realize that what you've found is more suited to your needs than what you thought you were looking for."
- Lawrence Block

Microbial Serendipity

I didn't know anyone personally who made kefir. I didn't know anyone who even knew what kefir was. I didn't know anyone who was trying to heal gut problems who could give me advice. The way I discovered kefir was actually through my husband. He brought up the dairy-free thing at work, and one of his co-workers piped up and said his wife also had to cut dairy while breastfeeding each of their five children—yes, five. Supposedly, she did this for the full year of breastfeeding for each of her kids.

   Call me crazy, but my first thought was that if this saint of a woman has five kids, then she must know what she was talking about. That instant trust, even for a woman I had never met before and one whom I knew nothing about, was both peculiar and real. After a few more conversations, my husband's co-worker and his wife gave us a little more advice: try one more thing while implementing a diary free diet—

   Kefir.

"Sounds weird," I thought, "Never heard of it."

Turned out that this sweet, soft-spoken father of five was also battling colon cancer, and he had been making kefir for himself as well as for his wife.

With a recommendation like that, in addition to the fact that I'm all about trying new foods, I was ready to go. And when you're in the middle of turning your diet upside down, anything goes! I was at the point where if someone told me to spin upside down on my head five times while drinking Alka-Seltzer and chewing licorice at the same time, I would've done it. Everything with my health seemed so backwards at the time that I figured I might as well throw this weird kefir brew into the mix. Like I said, I was desperate.

Now, as a general rule, any relationship born of desperation (especially human relationships) won't end well. When you're in distress and reaching for anything on the shelf that offers relief, most of the time those things we reach for are full of empty promises and, in the worst cases, end up hurting us even more. Heck, I'm pretty sure that's how 90% of prescription drug manufacturers earn our business. But this time, for whatever reason, the opposite was true. It was truly serendipitous, in every sense of the word. It was one of those life experiences you never saw coming, but, in retrospect, can't imagine your life without.

While all this was going on, I was back at school teaching. I remember the day my husband emailed me the first web links on this weird new food. As soon as the first recess bell rang, I sat at a little, first grader-sized table and started reading while my students were outside. The temporary peace of my little classroom offered a funny little sanctuary for the development of my upcoming obsession.

I read the kefir article.

And then I read it again.

And again.

There was something so mesmerizing about the whole kefir concept—it just made sense! Everything about it just seemed right deep down in my gut (pun intended), in such a way that I just wanted to try it as soon as possible. I did some quick Google searches, and the testimonials I found online seemed authentically awesome …but not in the way that was too good to be true. I wasn't looking for a quick fix, or to lose fifty pounds in two weeks. I just wanted to feel better. And that message was the number one thing people were talking about online, repeated over and over again. People were truly healing themselves with this food. I couldn't believe I hadn't heard of it before. Suddenly, however, the pragmatist inside me starting firing off internal questions:

Was this thing a supplement?
No, not a supplement. Check.

Was someone selling me on something?
No. Check.

Was it a whole food?
Yes. Check.

Could it really help me?
Maybe, but I needed to read more.

A Sip of Faith

It seemed that the more I read about kefir, the more questions I had—but in a good way. The more I read about how kefir interacts with the gut, the further my reading turned to the microbiome, which eventually led me to the integrated connection between our gut and everything else! It was a little pebble that snowballed furiously down the mountain, turning into that avalanche that I couldn't ignore. I was soaking it all up, learning things that I had never heard of: the battle between good and bad bacteria, gut-healing foods, probiotics, prebiotics. It was all so new!

After about two days of incessant reading—it finally clicked: I had a gut problem! Specifically, I had a gut bacteria problem.

It was a huge lightbulb moment. I finally had the answers I was searching for. Somewhere throughout the nine months of miserable vomiting and poor diet, my gut microbiome had changed. The damage done to my health and the trauma on my digestive system had altered the delicate microbial life balance in my gut—a microbiome that had been unscathed for my 27 years prior had been devastated. That's what was wrong with me! That's why I was feeling so crappy. That's why I now had food sensitivities, eczema, joint pain, foggy brain, constipation, depression, excessive tiredness, etc. All of this happened because there was something fundamentally (bacterially) different about me on an unseen, microscopic level. It was such a relief to know that all these things weren't just postpartum symptoms! This wasn't just the new "mom bod" that I had to deal with. It was so helpful to be able to—finally—put a name to my issues.

One thing was for sure: I had to get my hands on some kefir. I didn't know what that meant at the beginning, but I knew I wanted the best kefir I could make—and fast.

I'll never forget the first time I strained my grains and brought a spoon full of kefir to my mouth. I had read about this stuff incessantly and now, here it was, an inch from my lips. I couldn't even commit to drinking a full glass because I was so worried about making myself sick. I had nothing to tell me if the milk had spoiled or if it had turned to kefir, so I took a deep breath and swallowed a sip of faith.

I just had to trust the process, trust that the kefir grains were actually filling my milk with good bacteria instead of bad. I didn't know the science when I began, but it sure would have been helpful for someone to explain how the kefir grains changed the pH of the milk, killing off the bad bacteria. I would have loved for someone to tell me how much to drink and when to drink it. When you have eaten a canned, sterile diet your whole life, eating bacteria on purpose is kind of a big deal! Drinking warm, fermented milk full of purposefully grown bacteria required a paradigm shift of sorts. I knew in that moment that I had to start thinking about things—my health—differently.

Chapter Three

A New Perspective

"People have a hard time letting go of their suffering. Out of a fear of the unknown, they prefer suffering that is familiar."
-Thich Nhat Hanh

Why Did I Write This Book?

I wrote this book because I found something that organically changed my view about health. I'm not talking about organic foods, like that pricey section of the grocery store. The organic I'm talking about is fundamental—a change in how I view my health at the very root of the word. I'm going to tell you how I came to this paradigm shift. But first, I want to explain how this change occurred. Because my undergraduate degree is in Early Childhood Education, I'm going to use an educational theory to describe it.

Jean Piaget was a cognitive theorist. He believed that young children learn about the world in two ways: assimilation and accommodation. Assimilation is what kids do to pick up information that fits into the ideas they have about their world—called schemas. For example, a child may know about dogs. D-o-g. Dogs are furry animals with four legs. This child knows this because their family's pet dog is a Golden Retriever. But the first time this child encounters a Chihuahua (instead of a large, long-haired golden dog), the child must assimilate that dogs can be big or small. They have new information to fit into their schema. This child now knows that dogs can have long hair or short hair. Their d-o-g schema now fits a variety of dogs. Accommodation, on the other hand, is when a child must change their viewpoint because their new idea or experience doesn't fit in that category. For example, the first time that child sees a cat, he/she might call this four-legged creature a dog. When corrected, they have to create a new category in their mind for "cats." Cats make a "meow" sound and have prickly tongues and don't play fetch. All that information is put into a different drawer in the filing system within their brain.

We know that children can adjust their thinking very easily, almost daily. Adults, however, are quite a different story.

When was the last time you accommodated new information? When was a time when you really learned something new? Sometimes, as adults, we call it an "epiphany" or a describe it as a lightbulb moment. But, be honest—when was the last time you had a realization about your world that gave you a brand-new perspective? Stop and think for a minute. Does anything come to mind? Unfortunately, adults don't accommodate new information very often. Not only do we have enough world experience that we assume our understanding is substantial enough, but our minds are a lot more rigid. We reject things that don't fit into our schemas. We don't like to change our minds.

My recent accommodation came to me when I learned about kefir. Kefir forced me to develop a brand new idea about food—what healthy foods are actually all about. By accepting kefir as a new part of my life, I created an entire new schema called "cultured foods." It was weird and different, but it made so much sense to me! I had no idea that fermented foods existed outside of sauerkraut and knew even less about how these foods support the bacteria in our guts.

In fact, prior to kefir, I had no idea that most bacteria in our world is harmless. They are on, and in, everything around us. They live in me, on me, in the foods I eat, and surround everything I touch. My schema of bacteria was that they are simply "bad." Bacteria is BAD and dangerous, right? Isn't that what we've been told our whole lives? It was as if I had put on a new pair of lenses to see the world differently—the part of the world that revolves around those friendly microbes.

It was because of this new perspective that I suddenly realized that, if I wanted to be healthy, I had to follow the rules of biology; I had to follow the rules of nature that dictate our lives. If I wanted to be healthy, I had to work with the biology of my body. It was obvious to me that I had a gut problem and that my microbiome needed fixing. To do that, I had to follow the rules that sustained the life systems of these cells. To nourish these systems inside me, I had to follow their laws.

Kefir just happened to fall into my lap and created that bridge between my microbiome and my goals of fixing my health. It was through kefir that I learned and discovered everything I just described. It was with kefir that I learned to ferment my own foods and enjoy the benefits of a balanced and healthy gut. Kefir was the doorway through which I became exposed to an entirely new concept of health.

To Get Something You Never Had

Thomas Jefferson once said, "To get something you've never had, you must do something you've never done." I'll change this great quote just a smidge by saying this: sometimes, to get something we never had, we must be willing to look at it from a different perspective. I believe, more now than ever, that part of that change must begin with our perceptions—our paradigms—about health and fitness. That will lead to behavior changes that will have the greatest impact on our lives.

Sometimes people get the idea in their head that, in order to be healthy, they need to do "X." And they keep trying to do "X" but keep failing. They have really great intentions, but they always fall short. "X" just doesn't work, but they keep trying (and failing) because that's what they've been told (over and over again) will make them healthy. For years I thought if I just run more, I will be in shape. "It's great cardio and excellent for your health!" they say. But the truth is—I am a terrible runner. I have short legs and a stocky build. The only enjoyment I get out of it is the challenge. It's simply not "my thing." Do I run? Yes, sometimes. But it is not part of my fundamental health routine. For others, I can totally see how running may be an absolutely essential component of their personal fitness, but it didn't exactly match for me. So, I can try and try and try to run, but it will never be the thing to transform my health.

What I'm saying is, while you read this book, be open to believing something new about what it means to be healthy and to eat healthy foods.

Here's what I believe: Food is good. We need healthy foods to live. Food is also healing. In some ways, it can be as transformative as a doctor's prescription—perhaps even more transformative! And now we know that the healthy, vital bacteria in our guts also needs food to live. Instead of feeding our endless appetite, how about we feed the gut? If we feed the body, the body will be kind in return. We will feel better when we listen to our body, NOT mainstream health advice. Throw away those magazines, people! Stop eating processed foods that damage the body. START eating foods that fuel the gut and you will discover that they fuel your body on a complete, whole level.

That second part is the key to success. We start to feel good when we quit eating processed, cheap, fake food. What makes you feel great though, is fueling your gut and body with healthy foods. Fruits and vegetables, foods particularly rich in prebiotics, grains, fermented foods like kefir, and other nutrient-dense foods that fuel your body will make you feel great.

You're probably thinking, "Ok, so I should eat healthy foods… great, never heard that one before…" I get it. Part of that sounds like what you've heard your entire life. But, look with me just one step further. Instead of just saying "I need to eat healthy," try shifting your schema to, "What can I eat that will feed my gut and make me feel better?" It sounds simple, I know, but this is where I'm asking you to take a little dose of humility for that adult mind of yours and begin to shift your personal schema, just a bit.

Don't worry, schema shifting doesn't hurt nearly as bad as being a presumptuous pain in the ass does, especially in the long term.

Remember: Your Gut Has Everything to Do with How You Feel.

Why Aren't People Really Talking about Kefir?

Now, I'll tell you the second reason I wrote this book. Prior to our Spring-born baby, I spent six fantastic years teaching in the public school system. I taught first and second grades in gifted education. But as soon as I got those sweet baby cheeks cuddled in my arms, nothing else mattered. Together, we made the decision that I would stay home to raise our daughter. So I finished out the school year and stayed home thereafter. It was the right decision for us, but the change of pace really threw me for a loop. I am ridiculously good at keeping busy, but I felt very tied down as a new stay-at-home mom. In order to save my sanity, I knew I needed to do something:

Write a book.

I was itching to answer the question: Why was no one really talking about kefir? Why was nobody making it themselves? Why isn't it everywhere?!

The first answer came when I started researching. I was fascinated at a food so complex. Each day, I uncovered another layer. It was like an onion. It just kept peeling layer after layer. In the beginning of my research, kefir went from "a drinkable yogurt" to "a traditional fermented milk drink" to "gut-healing, uniquely cultured probiotic drink you can easily make yourself" by the end. But the digging just never stopped. It's not like other health foods I love. With kefir, the more I read, the more questions I had about my health. The more I searched, the more I realized that nobody else seemed to be talking about kefir—at least, the general public wasn't talking about kefir.

What I discovered is that ALL of the best information about kefir was found in scientific articles! All that research wasn't on any single website, it wasn't in any books. All this rich information about kefir was hiding under the dome of some academic Hufflepuff. Further, whatever layman information that was out there on the internet for the grabbing, was contradictory to the other information. But, all of it was clarified in the research. And no one was bringing that research out to the public eye!

Another reason why nobody is talking about kefir? When there's an elephant in the room—introduce it. I'll be the first one to say it… kefir is weird! It is weird and unorthodox (well, at least to our modern diet). "Fermented" anything just sounds terrible, let alone fermented milk. Milk is supposed to be that nicely chilled creamy drink that you dip cookies in. You've probably loved it since you were a child (whether or not you drink it today). You've been told all your life that milk will "sour" when you leave it at room temperature. I get it. I felt all the same things when I was learning about kefir, too. I'll tell ya, the struggle is real! But after my first batch of kefir, I was hooked. Hopefully, you will be too!

This is why kefir is gaining a following of people. This is why people drink it regularly and LOVE it. People wouldn't jump over that "warm milk" idea if they didn't feel a direct benefit. People are motivated to try something new or change something in their life if they can feel the benefits.

Of all the things I've uncovered about kefir, the foundational element that I keep going back to is this:

Kefir is NOT new. It has been a miraculous source of healing for thousands of years. Kefir is time-proven. It's not a pill or powder manufactured to "meet your every need." It heals naturally. My goal is to describe kefir as a therapeutic food that will do much more for your health than you think it will. My goal is to make kefir simple. My goal is to convince you that it's really not as weird as you think it is. If you can just get over that "warm milk" thing, I promise you will begin to uncover the layers of your health, too.

Starting to feel your schema shift, at least a little bit? Nah… couldn't be. It's probably just gas…

Chapter Four

Behind Your Belly Button

"Every day we live, and every meal we eat, we influence the great microbial organ inside us—for better or for worse."
- Giulia Enders

Your Gut Is Like a Black Box

Unless you're a gastroenterologist, you probably don't have a regular, first-hand perspective of what happens inside your gut (sigmoidoscopes aren't exactly common bathroom appliances). For most of us, the closest we ever come to "looking" inside our gut is staring at our naval in the mirror. We can feel it rumble when we're hungry, we can feel it bloat when we're gassy, and often we feel pain for a variety of reasons, but never do we truly see our gut. And because of that, it's like a black box, sitting there in the middle of our bodies. We put something in, some "stuff" happens in the middle, and then something (poop) comes out the other end.

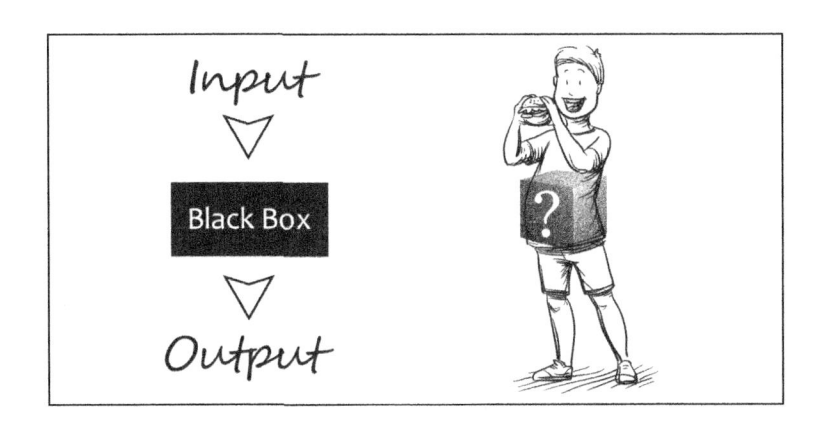

Until recently, this is the way I viewed digestion. You just put stuff into your mouth, something "happened" in the gut, and out came poop. And it took place the same way every time I digested any of my food. I used to think that digestion was just digestion, and I didn't know what it looked like, how it worked, and frankly—I didn't care. Digestion was just your regular day in-day out "stomach stuff." I just kind of thought that the only function of the gut was to be the middle man— the thing in charge of turning food into ... poop.

Sound like a black box to you, too?

Many people haven't the slightest clue what goes on inside our guts. Consequently, many people don't take care of their gut health and don't give it a passing glance (unless you "shart," then you will definitely give it a glance). It's like that saying, "You don't know what you don't know." If you don't know anything about how your gut works, then how are you supposed to take care of it?

Gut 101

The "gut" is basically the digestive system. Anything our food touches after it's swallowed is considered to be "the gut." This includes our mouth, esophagus, stomach, small intestines, colon, and rectum.

The gut is a fascinating organ system. Its main job, obviously, is to break down the food we eat and absorb those nutrients, acids, fats, and water. And, its most-often overlooked function, aside from digestion, is that it also acts as a central hub for many vital systems in our body. Think of it like a train station. Many different body systems interact together through the central gut "station." The heart, brain, and endocrine systems (hormones) all team up in the gut to get their respective jobs done. The gut also plays a critical role in our immune system, helps regulate the nervous system, and is a central location for hormone production.

Here's an interesting fact, though: Even though the gut is connected to all of these other body systems, it is actually quite independent. What I mean is, our gut does its job even without the rest of the body. It continues to work even when other body systems shut down. It is even possible if your brain is in a vegetative state and foods are delivered directly to the stomach (through a tube) for digestion to still take place. Even for a paraplegic person who does not have control of the majority of their body, digestion will still function normally. Maybe that's why it's so easy for us to ignore it, because it has such a fantastic auto-pilot—but that can be a blessing and a curse.

"So you're saying it's both interrelated to all other body systems, but can still function independently?"

Exactly.

Interesting Facts About the Gut:

- The small intestine is about 20 feet long.
- The large intestine is about 5 feet long.
- The surface area of the inside of your gut is the size of a tennis court.

- Every square inch of the of your gut lining is covered with 20,000 nutrient receptors.
- The acid in your stomach is strong enough to burn your skin.
- The gut produces much more serotonin and dopamine than your brain does.
- Everybody expels about 1-4 liters of gas a day (yes, even you, sweetheart!).
- The esophagus can contract/relax food into the stomach, even when you're upside down.
- 60% of your stool comprises bacteria (alive and dead).
- A French kiss can transfer up to 80 million harmless microbes from mouth to mouth.

Do You Have a Gut Problem?

We just don't think about the condition of our gut unless we are forced to. It's the same reason we don't think about the roof above our head unless we have a leaky puddle in our living room. If things seem to be working, we don't think about them. Once they are broken, however, those "symptoms" suddenly demand our attention.

The funny thing is, for a lot of people, those symptoms have to get pretty severe in order to grab our attention. I hear this a lot: "Oh, I don't have a gut problem… I just have an upset stomach all the time", "Oh, I don't have digestion problems, I just get diarrhea every time I eat fruit", or "My gut is fine, I just have an irritable bowel."

Sound familiar?

Sorry to break it to you, babe: You've got a gut problem. Even the smallest change in digestion can be an indication of what's going on inside our gut. Have you ever wondered about the following?

- Why am I bloated?
- What is causing my constipation? Diarrhea? Heartburn? Nausea?
- Why does my stomach get upset after eating certain foods?
- What can I do about embarrassing gas?
- How do I know if I have inflammation?
- Why am I depressed or moody?
- How can I go another night without sleep?
- I have an autoimmune disease… what does this have to do with my gut?

If you find yourself asking these kinds of questions on more than one occasion, then it's time for some answers. Of course, there is no single diagnostic test to determine the health of our gut. We can't draw your blood and say "yes" or "no" as to whether your gut is healthy or not. There is no black and white. The fact of the matter is, your gut is unique to you and so are its associated health considerations. However, it is possible to "read into" certain aspects of your health that may give you a clue as to what is causing problems.

And, while we're on the subject, let's expand our vocabulary a little bit. Before reading this book, I would venture to guess that you've probably heard the term "gut" before. It's fairly common, people talk about it from time to time. Well, let me throw another term at you that is less widely known, yet fundamentally important in understanding gut health:

"Microbiome"

Have you heard of it? Whether you have or not, get acquainted with the it, because you've got one, and chances are you're probably don't know how to take care of it.

I know I didn't. Let's talk about why.

Chapter Five

Microbiome & Dysbiosis

"One day we will have an understanding of what each microbe in everybody's microbial signature actually means. Therefore, we can test early on to correct any dysfunction that any one individual may have."
- Deanna L. Gibson, Ph.D.

What Is A "Microbiome?"

Micro: small
Biome: naturally occurring community, or habitat

A microbiome is a colony of bacteria that have created a home inside your gut. Your gut is their ecosystem. These single-celled microorganisms line the tissues of your entire gut, but are most highly concentrated within the large intestine, or colon. About 90% of your gut microbes "hang out" in your large intestine—it's where they do most of their work.

Fair warning: this is going to get a little "science-y," but put your nerd glasses on and stick with me, it'll be good for ya. I promise.

Your microbiome is sometimes referred to as the "second genome," meaning it is unique enough to identify you outside of your actual DNA genetics. It's not quite like DNA, though.

For example, I am 100% guaranteed to have a DNA makeup consisting of portions of my parent's DNA. As such, both of my sisters possess similar genetic "code" gifted to them by our shared parents. However, my microbiome could be quite different than my parents' and siblings'. The uniqueness of your microbiome is the result of many things, including genetics, the food you eat, the places you live, and the people you surround yourself with. They all have bacteria, too, you know! As I'll explain later, your microbiome changes throughout your life, starting from the day you were born until the day you die. So, even though your microbiome is completely unique to you, it can—and will—change.

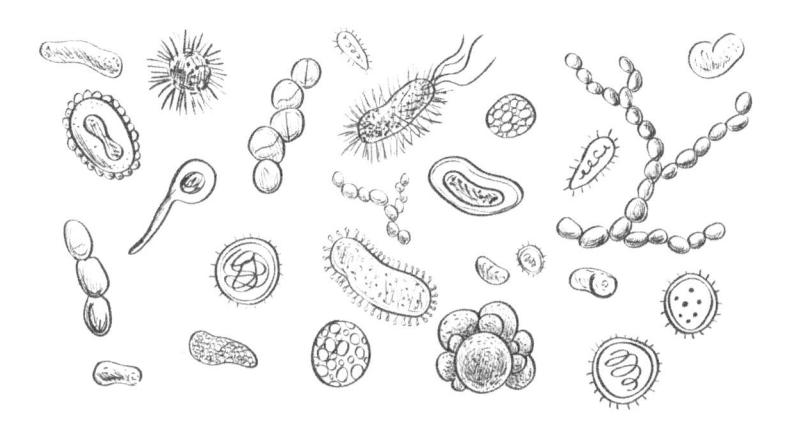

Here's another way of looking at it. Let's say that your gut is like New York City, a sprawling and immense metropolis buzzing with life. Its streets are alive with movement—a city that never sleeps; always alive, both day and night. Picture its famous skyline: the buildings, bridges, and landmarks. Think of those buildings like your organ systems. They are part of you—they are your body. Now, with your mind's eye, zoom in a little closer. The city streets are full of people: in cars, on bikes, on foot, running around from work, to school, in and out of restaurants, etc. These New Yorkers—these people—think of them like the bacteria of your gut. They are, themselves, their own little organisms living, by the millions, inside you; but technically, they aren't you—they just live with you. And, just like New York, this large and busy population is incredibly diverse. In fact, the more diverse the population, the healthier the city.

Now, for most people, when they think about their guts, they only think about the buildings (the organs), they fail to realize that without the life blood (the bacteria) which inhabits and animates those buildings, the city (your body) would no function fully and would eventually fade away. It's this relationship—this combination of organs and bacteria—that make up a happy, healthy, and diverse microbiome.

How Your Microbiome Became Unique

Babies in the womb are essentially isolated from bacteria. Their guts are "sterile" until they are delivered from the womb. All babies immediately begin collecting bacteria the instant they are born. As soon as the baby comes in contact with the world outside of the womb, it begins to collect bacteria. Even the way a baby is born affects the type of bacteria it collects. Babies delivered vaginally have very different microbes than those born via C-section[2]. The sources they collect bacteria from the moment they are born change their microbiome.

Babies born via the vaginal canal pick up their mother's bacteria as they swallow the fluid while passing through the birth canal. In fact, studies show that these vaginally born babies have much higher proportions of Lactobacillus, Prevotella, and Sneathia bacteria, which are similar to a mother's vaginal bacteria populations. On the other hand, babies born via C-section have higher proportions of bacteria that resemble the skin bacteria of the other people in the delivery room, such as Staphylococcus, Corynebacterium, and Propionibacterium. Consequently, a baby born in a hospital will have different bacteria than, say, a baby born at home or in the back seat of a Buick.

And, it's important to remember, bacteria isn't a bad thing. It's a necessary fact of life.

Further, a significant difference has been shown between microbiomes of babies fed breast milk and those fed formula[3]. Breastfed infants have a much more robust and diverse bacteria count, while those who are formula-fed are less bacterially diverse. This is due to the fact that breastmilk features natural bacteria produced by the mother's body, as well as inulin (complex sugars) that help feed that bacteria. Formula is able to meet all the nutritional components required for babies, like proteins, fats, and nutrients, but it fundamentally lacks the living components to fuel the growth of healthy, organic bacteria.

What does this mean, you ask? I am very well aware that not all mothers have a choice in sensitive medical situations that dictate where or how their baby is born. Nor are all mothers able or wanting to breastfeed. The point is simply that these studies inform us about how significant the environment, and what we eat as mothers, is to an infant's microbiome—especially since they are developing their own unique, bacterial identity.

The first few months of life aren't the only thing that matters when it comes to our microbiome, however. As life continues, the microbiome collects bacteria from all kinds of sources. Your microbiome collects bacteria from, and is affected by, nearly everything you do, including:

- The food you eat and the water you drink.
- Pets or animals you interact with closely.
- Whether you live in the country or the city.
- Your housing arrangements.
- Whether you're predominantly active or inactive.

- If you spend most of your time indoors or outdoors.
- Your stress level.

It's all connected and it's all affected. It's constantly changing. It changes literally every day. Your microbiome is the very definition of dynamic.

To illustrate the impact of environment, one study looked at the shared microbes in families with and without pets. The families without pets had more bacteria in common with each other[4]. They looked similar to each other. Those with pets displayed more diverse microbe populations—they were less similar to the other humans in their home—suggesting that the simple the presence of a pet in your house can change the microbial environment enough to change your gut.

Several other studies show that your microbiome can change with your geographical location and the food and cultural mixing that it entails[5]. One study tracked a group of rural African tribe members with a primarily plant-based diet who then immigrated to a city in Italy. Not surprisingly, their microbiomes changed significantly and, over time, they more closely resembled the native Italians. Their housing situation, people they were surrounded by, and their diet changed, and so did their microbiome.

Your gut will continue to be unique and evolve through each stage of your life as well. As you age, the choices of food, lifestyle, and other factors will continuously shape your microbiome. This is even true for pregnant women whose individual microbial populations evolve through the various stages of pregnancy. In short, your microbiome changes with your body as you move through the stages of pregnancy.

What this is telling us is that the world revolves around a hidden ecosystem of microbial communities. We can't see them, but they are there and are constantly changing.

You may be asking, "Why do we care?"

Remember: Your Gut Has Everything to Do With How You Feel.

A Microscopically Diverse World

Just as there are various species of plants and animals, there are an estimated 10,000+ strains of bacteria commonly found in the human gut! Interestingly enough, it's estimated that only about 50 strains are common among MOST of the human population around the world. That means you and I have many of the same bacteria, but could also be very different, depending upon the combinations thereof.

Here is a list of some commonly found genera of bacteria (these are some of the "good guys"):

- Bacteriodes
- Clostridium
- Faecalibacterium
- Eubacterium
- Ruminococcus
- Peptococcus
- Peptostreptococcus
- Bifidobacterium
- Escherichia
- Lactobacillus

Sounds like a bunch of scientific mumbo jumbo, I know. But the discovery of many of these different species of bacteria is actually quite new and exciting. Prior to 2002, any study or analysis on bacteria had to be done with a Petri dish and an old fashioned microscope. With the development of new technology, however, scientists have been able to sequence bacterial DNA. What this means is that now they can take a mouth swab of a person, ship it across the country, and they can analyze a person's microbes by looking at the microbial DNA, which is not dependent upon looking at the actual live culture through a microscope.

Translation? Tiny samples = lots of usable, complete data regarding a person's microbiome health very quickly.

This is also why we are just learning about the gut and gut health. With this newfound ability of bacterial analysis, we're breaking new ground in understanding what makes us feel the way we do, along with where many of our common diseases stem from. Eventually, the goal of the future would be to use our individual microbial identity to treat and prevent disease.

Dysbiosis (aka Disease)

Dys: bad, or difficult
Biosis: state of life

You can see, right of the bat, that having an unhealthy microbiome quite literally means, "difficult way to live life." So, let's talk about how things with our gut start to go south on us, and how that leads to sickness, disease, discomfort, and pain.

One thing we know for sure is that your gut needs to have much more good bacteria than bad bacteria. Naturally, your gut consists of about 85% good bacteria and about 15% bad (or pathogenic) bacteria[6]. This is a typical ratio and it's okay to have some bad bacteria in your gut—it's normal. Remember our New York example? The good bacteria is constantly working against the bad bacteria to keep it in check. Think of it like a never-ending battleground. The good bacteria is constantly on the front line holding back the bad bacteria. You know, like a Batman vs. the Joker kind of a thing.

Just like all living things, bacteria eat, poop, and reproduce. The bacteria inside your body eat whatever you eat by absorbing it through their cellular membrane. This means that the foods you eat directly affect your microbiome. Healthy foods like kefir and foods rich in prebiotics provide food for the good bacteria and helps them thrive. Simple sugars and some types of yeasts provide food for the bad bacteria.

When the bad bacteria grows too powerful, illness or harm is done to the body. This is something called dysbiosis. Dysbiosis is a change in the gut flora (microbe population) that results in the microbiota producing harmful effects for the body. Some of these harmful effects are largely variant, but may include inflammation, auto-immune disorders, and more. Some of the common, harmful bacteria strains might sound familiar: clostridia, streptococci, staphylococci, listeria, legionella, e. Coli, etc.

According to the American Nutrition Association, symptoms of dysbiosis can include[7]:

- Fatigue
- Poor memory or Spacey feeling
- Insomnia and Hypersomnia
- Anxiety or Depression
- Mood swings
- Muscle and joint aches and pains
- Alcohol intolerance
- Itching
- Frequent urination
- Skin rash
- Palpitations
- Gas or bloating
- Diarrhea or Constipation
- Candida

- Body odors and bad breath
- Eczema
- Psoriasis
- Frequent colds

...and that's not even a comprehensive list.

Are you starting to see how your gut has everything to do with how you feel?

Recipe for Repair

There is hope in healing. As you might imagine, the gut isn't something that can be healed overnight. With that being said, most people are surprised by how quickly they begin to start feeling better once they actually start paying attention to the "black box" behind their belly button. Often, just drinking a single cup of homemade kefir per day is enough to cause real change in as little as seven days. And, while we'll spend the rest of the book going into detail regarding what kefir is, how to make it, and what it will do for you, here are some general principles for gut health and repair:

1. Remove: Remove harmful substances and toxins from your body that could cause damage to your gut. Of course, everybody will be different here, but these might include things like sugar, sugar alcohols, processed foods, food allergens, antibiotics, NSAIDS (when not necessary), stress, alcohol, caffeine, and even some medications, such as birth control. This may include working closely with your physician to identify and treat any pre-existing infections in the body.

2. Replace: Replace the removed substances with healing foods. Healing foods are prebiotic-rich foods, foods with dense nutrition, fermented dairy and veggies, sprouted

seeds, essential fatty acids, omega-3 foods found in things like salmon, chia, and hemp seeds, and others. If stomach acid and digestive enzymes are not in proper function, these also need replenishing.

3. Repair: Repair your gut lining, if needed, with supplements. A few examples of this might be digestive enzymes, glutamine, licorice root, or quercetin. I recommend only taking these under the supervision of a dietitian or medical professional. These are needed on a case-by-case basis and are not for everyone.

4. Rebalance with probiotics: You can get probiotics from, of course, kefir, other fermented dairy products like yogurt, fermented vegetables, kombucha, and more. If you can get probiotics in the form of real food, then eat probiotic-rich foods. If you can get vitamins and minerals from fruits and veggies, then get them from fruits and veggies first. THEN and only if you feel it is needed, you can take other supplements.

Now that we've introduced you to those lovely little bugs living inside you, let's talk about what they can do for you.

Chapter Six

Probiotics and Prebiotics

"A growing body of scientific evidence suggests that you can treat and prevent some illnesses with... certain kinds of health-promoting bacteria, called probiotics."
-Harvard Medical School

What the Hell Is a Probiotic, Anyway?

You've seen the yogurt commercials. You've been exposed to the marketing. You've heard of probiotics. If you're like I was, you're vaguely aware that probiotics are good for you, but aren't really sure exactly what they are or how they work. Let's start by working past the buzzword.

Probiotic means "pro-life." Probiotics are living organisms. They are single-celled bacteria. When they are consumed by the host (i.e., us), they benefit the health of the host. Plain and simple. Probiotics are living organisms that benefit our health.

However, there is a huge gap between the science of probiotics and how people actually use them in their daily lives. On one hand, there is the scientific evidence behind probiotics. Scientists have used DNA sequencing to learn all about these living organisms and have documented how they can significantly benefit our health. On the other hand, there is the general population who consumes these products but aren't sure why. Moreover, our population's consumption and use of probiotics is driven more by marketing than it is by empirical evidence. Most people are under the impression that anything labeled "probiotic" will provide some benefits, but when pressed about what those benefits are, shrugged shoulders are often the response.

Because probiotics are a trendy topic right now in the health market, you can find just about anyone selling or purchasing probiotics, usually in supplement form. Of the more inquisitive probiotic parishioners, after doing a little reading, there seems to be a never-ending list of questions surrounding these products. Are they all created equal? Does it matter if I eat the classic yogurt with live cultures or just take a pill? What about these powders and capsules? Can I just get any box of probiotics at my local grocery store and call it good?

Time to clear the air.

According to research, there are two requirements for a probiotic, when consumed, to actually benefit your health.

1. Probiotics must be consumed as living organisms to be effective.

Dead organisms don't do anything—they're dead. It's like bringing home a goldfish from the pet store only to find out that it died on the car ride home. For your six-year-old who may be seeking mini, marine life companionship in the form of a fish, a floater won't do the trick. Probiotics are no different. (You didn't know you were getting parenting advice along with all of this probiotic talk, did you?) Remember: Dead = Doesn't Work.

2. Probiotics must reach the intestines to have positive health effects.

That means probiotics must make it past the stomach alive and hang out with the bacteria in the large intestine to be effective. Think of it like sunscreen for our skin. It's like squirting a dose of sunscreen onto your hands, but not actually applying it over your body. If sunscreen doesn't cover your skin, it doesn't protect it from the sun. Likewise, if probiotics don't travel to the gut alive, they can't be effective. The large intestine is the target destination for the probiotics.

So yeah, the kind of probiotic you use, and where you get it from, matters. Not all probiotics are created equal. I see this all the time: a company will advertise something as a probiotic, but it either doesn't have ANY live-active cultures or may contain a dismal amount. To really get the benefits of probiotics, the cultures must be living. It only makes sense that to fill your gut with a living, vibrant, beneficial, bacterial community it must be living. MANY popular yogurts at your local grocery store are not going to have live cultures. Many probiotic pills don't have living cultures in them, or they may be freeze dried. I don't know about you, but when I hear the words "freeze dried," I don't exactly think of life, vibrancy, or health.

Another crucial element to taking probiotics is to look at the number of them you'll be getting. How many bacteria in one dose? This number is reported as colony-forming units (CFUs), which is the density of bacteria in the product. Knowing the concentration is important if you think about how many trillions of bacteria are in your gut—ten trillion to be exact—all of which comprises a thousand different strains. If a product has less than 15-100 billion units, then it will hardly make a noticeable impact on your gut. Also, look for probiotics that contain more than ten strains, preferably upwards of thirty strains. The tricky thing about this is that many products won't tell you. One of my favorite yogurt brands contains two live active cultures, but neither the label or the website advertises the CFU. Even if a product does label the CFU, it may be deceiving.

I once bought a probiotic drink at the grocery store similar to kefir that advertised "One billion probiotics per serving," which, to the average Joe, would sound like a lot, right? "Wow, one billion!" But when you compare one billion to the ten trillion found in kefir, that's 0.0001%. On top of that, there was a whopping seventeen grams of sugar in every serving of that drink. No thanks, "probiotic" drink. Not worth it. Next time you see a drink like that in your local grocery store, I'd recommend brushing your shoulder off and moving on to the next aisle.

The last thing to look out for is how the probiotics are delivered. Is it in the form of a pill that has added chemicals? A powder with fillers? I personally believe that anytime you can get nutritional needs from REAL FOOD, then that's what you should do. Real food with nutritional benefits (vitamins, minerals, calories, fiber, etc.) trumps pills or powders—every time.

Prebiotics

Prebiotics are another element of nutrition that is very misunderstood and little known. That's right, I said "pre"-biotics. Not pro. Prebiotics are a type of carbohydrate that is not digested by your system. You can chew and chew and chew, and your body can try to digest it, but it is not absorbed. It merely passes on through to the large intestine.

Remember the large concentration of microbes in your large intestine? When these prebiotics reach the microbe communities, the bacteria starts to feed on these prebiotics for growth and survival. Your body doesn't consume them—the bacteria does. Think of prebiotics as fertilizer. Fertilizer doesn't grow new grass. It feeds the existing grass and makes it rich and healthy. Likewise, prebiotics feed the good bacteria that already exist in your gut. It helps the good bacteria grow strong and robust.

Prebiotics come mainly from vegetables and other fibrous foods. The recommendation is to eat about 5-8 grams a day. This is equivalent to about a cup of jicama, which is a food highly dense in prebiotics. They are also found in common foods like milk, bananas, wheat, and oats. Unfortunately, prebiotics are not something you will find on nutrition labels.

As a general rule, make sure to eat plenty of vegetables and other foods in the list below.

Prebiotic Foods:

- Jicama
- Jerusalem artichoke
- Chicory root
- Dandelion greens
- Allium vegetables (Garlic, Onion, Chives, etc.)
- Whole grain and sprouted-grain breads
- Wheat germ, whole wheat berries
- Avocado
- Peas
- Soybeans
- Potato skins
- Organic apple cider vinegar

Prebiotics are different than other carbohydrates in that other carbohydrates (sugars and starches) are broken down beginning in the stomach, are consumed in the small intestine, and are then sent to your bloodstream. This in turn affects your blood sugar levels. If it's not used as energy, then it is stored as glycogen (and sometimes excess fat). Prebiotics, on the other hand, never enter your bloodstream and thus, can be considered a zero calorie substance! Don't get too excited though, because the foods listed above aren't technically zero calories, just the prebiotics themselves.

Sad, I know.

Let's demonstrate the effects of this: Do you know what the difference is between green bananas and ripe, brown bananas? Green bananas are less sweet and are sometimes even a little firm. Brown bananas turn soft and become very sweet. You may have your preference, but when it comes to the gut, green bananas have more of those prebiotic fibers to feed the bacteria inside you. A green banana has those indigestible carbohydrates that feed the gut bacteria. As the banana ripens, however, those carbohydrates are turned into simple sugars. That's why you use ripe bananas when you cook, such as in banana bread. The ripe banana contains a simpler sugar structure that is quickly absorbed into the bloodstream, while the ripe banana won't spike your blood sugar levels.

Another rich source of prebiotics is breast milk. Breast milk, believe it or not, contains a prebiotic. It's a certain carbohydrate called an oligosaccharide that promotes healthy baby bellies. This may be a contributing factor as to why breastfeed babies have fewer infections, asthma, and allergies than formula-fed babies[8]. One researcher even confirmed that, when formula-fed babies had an added dose of prebiotics in their formula, their stools displayed greater amounts of bifidobacteria, which greater mimicked breast-fed babies[9].

Putting two and two together, more bacteria in the stool means more bacteria in the digestive system, which indicates healthier gut flora. Chalk up another point for prebiotics.

Lucky for you, kefir has it all! Fermented milk products are great because they have prebiotics AND probiotics in them, making them symbiotic. Kefir has both the bacteria richness and the fuel to get it to our large intestine. Milk is the perfect vehicle to get the probiotics to the gut. It can pass through the stomach acid mostly unscathed. Remember how probiotics need a vehicle to bypass the acidity of the stomach? Cultured dairy is really effective in delivering probiotics to the gut because dairy has the ability to coat the stomach. This blocks part of the acidic nature of the stomach from killing the probiotics. Cultured dairy also contains the food for the bacteria along the way to deliver it to the large intestine nice and healthy.

Let's compare the differences between pre & pro:

Prebiotic: Carbohydrates that feed good bacteria
Probiotic: Living colony of good bacteria

Prebiotic: Comes mostly from vegetables
Probiotic: Exists in your gut, supplemented with foods and other live cultures

Prebiotic: Temperature does not need to be regulated for these foods
Probiotic: Sensitive to temperature (can be killed with heat)

Prebiotic: When consumed, feeds the good bacteria, promoting healthy growth
Probiotic: When consumed, adds diverse strains of probiotics

Chapter Seven

Digestion

"Digestion, of all the bodily functions, is the one which exercises the greatest influence on the mental state of an individual."
- Jean-Anthelme Brillat-Savarin

Team Digestion

Are you familiar with those Pepto Bismol commercials on TV? If you're between the age of five and ninety years old, you've seen them. You know the jingle: "Nausea, Heartburn, Indigestion—Upset Stomach—Diarrhea!" repeated over and over again while people of various shapes and sizes dance around with weird looks on their faces. While I apologize for the fact that their pesky little jingle will now be stuck in your head for the next thirty minutes, I want to congratulate ol' Pepto for doing something that most people aren't willing to do: talk about digestion in public and, for that matter, doing it in a funny and memorable way (heck, somebody came up with a song about diarrhea—give that guy a medal!). So, in the spirit of that familiar pink slime, I want to pose a question:

Why don't more people talk about digestion?

I mean, I totally get the social appropriateness of not talking about your poop with certain groups of people. However, I think we should talk about it more—especially since seventy-plus million Americans have a diagnosed digestive disease.

Digestion is what makes your world turn round. It's what gives life and sustenance to your body. Your body's ability to digest is as important to you as the food you eat. When digestion doesn't function properly, the body is left malnourished, starving, weak, and diseased. Making sure your digestion is running in tip-top shape is fundamental to your health. Not only is it important from a nutritional standpoint, making sure you get key nutrients, but it is also important from an I-feel-good-every-day standpoint.

Digestion isn't as simple as "food goes in and poop comes out." It's far more complicated than that. Think about how your body needs to turn an apple into absorbable nutrients: it turns a piece of solid matter into cellular components! That apple has to transform from a whole food into micro-matter that can be absorbed into your bloodstream. It's remarkable that your body is working on this literally all day long!

The Gut

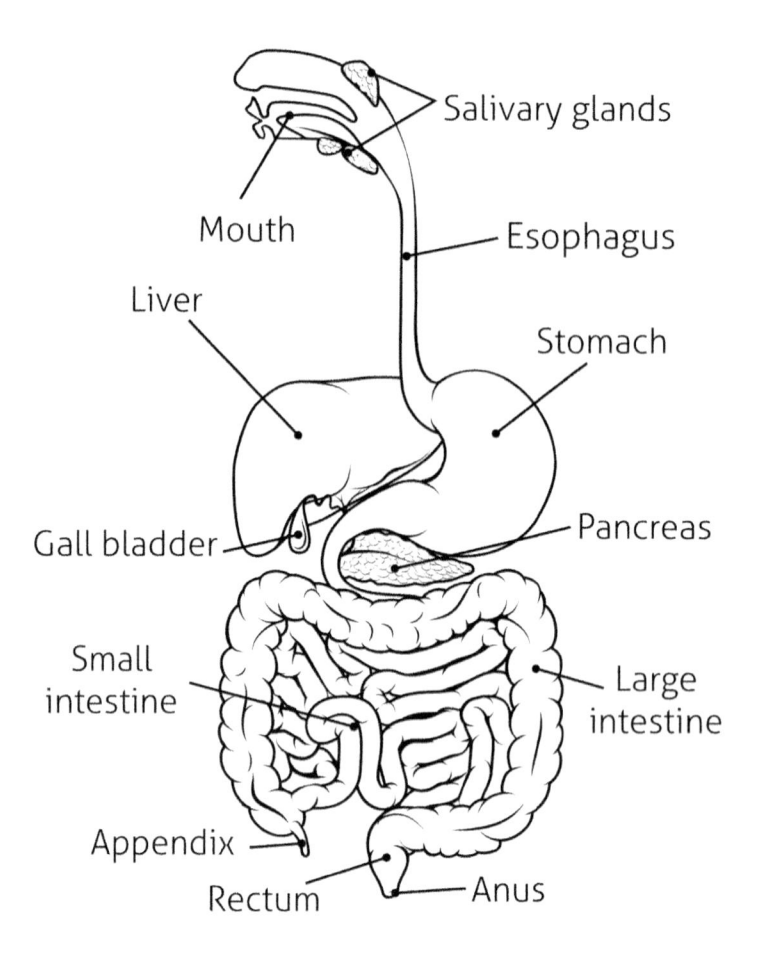

- Salivary glands
- Mouth
- Esophagus
- Liver
- Stomach
- Gall bladder
- Pancreas
- Small intestine
- Large intestine
- Appendix
- Rectum
- Anus

Role Players

These guys are like the Avengers, but instead of fighting intergalactic battles, they help you eat, poop, and stay alive.

The Brain: Usually we think of digestion in terms of "mouth to butthole," but you may be surprised to learn that the brain is the central processor for digestion. There is an extremely large nerve that connects straight from the brain to the gut that is called the vagus nerve. This nerve constantly receives sensory information from the gut. Since the gut works without our conscious thought, the brain is in charge of communicating those "I'm hungry" or "I'm full" messages. These never-ending signals seem to be the bane of our existence sometimes, but our life literally depends on them. If we don't eat, then we die, right? Further, and perhaps most important, the brain also triggers hormones once food enters our mouth to produce saliva, acids, and enzymes to digest our food.

Mouth and Esophagus: The mouth, obviously, is the entry point to digestion—where food starts breaking down into smaller bits. With the help of our teeth, the large food chunks get broken down into tiny particles. They grind and crush our food to make the next stage just a little bit easier. The food gets pushed down through the esophagus. It passes the upper esophageal sphincter (UES) and the lower esophageal sphincter (LES). The LES sits right on top of the stomach and is often the culprit for heartburn symptoms or gastroesophageal reflux disease (GERD). When this valve doesn't close all the way after the food passes, or opens by mistake, the acid form our stomach slips up through the esophagus, causing that nasty burning feeling.

Stomach: The stomach continues the breakdown of food. It does this mechanically by contracting muscles to churn the food into mush. It also releases those enzymes, mentioned earlier, to break down fats and acids to a smaller, molecular level. This process takes about 2-4 hours before the food is passed on to the next stage. Did you know that the only things absorbed into your body in the stomach are aspirin, alcohol, and water? Everything else is absorbed later in the intestines. The stomach is also on the forefront of immunity. It wards off bad pathogens with the stomach acid, or bile. The acid kills unwanted or harmful microorganisms and is strong enough to burn your skin (which is why heartburn feels so terrible). However, the stomach is protected with a coat of mucus that lubricates the stomach lining.

Small Intestine: The small intestine is where most of the food's nutrients are absorbed: calcium, vitamins, minerals, sugars, fatty acids, folate, folic acid, proteins, cholesterol, and salt are all absorbed here. This is the part of the gut where the gut mucosa, or gut lining, has huge implications for the nutrition we receive from our diet. This mucosa is covered with structures called villi. These finger-like projections have the job of absorbing all those nutrients I just mentioned. They drastically increase the surface area of the gut in order to absorb more nutrients as the mush of food passes by. Inflammation of the villi, or damaged villi, can lead to flattened structures and can severely decrease the body's ability to absorb any nutrition. The mucosal layer also has a layer of cells that bind together to keep out unwanted things like acid and food particles from entering the surrounding tissues and thus entering our blood stream. Losing the integrity of the gut is often referred to as Leaky Gut Syndrome (more on that in a bit).

Large Intestine: This is also called the colon. The main job of the colon is to absorb water and any other nutrients that pass through from the small intestine. Once most of the water is absorbed, it compacts the remains into stool. Your poop is comprised of undigested food, fiber, and bacteria—both alive and dead. In fact, 90% of the bacteria in your entire digestive system "hang out" in the colon. They collect on and in the tissues of the intestinal wall.

Accessory Organs: These organs don't technically touch food, but they do play a role in digestion. The liver produces bile to aid in fat digestion and absorption. The pancreas secretes sodium bicarbonate and releases enzymes to digest carbohydrates, fats, and proteins. Lastly, the gallbladder stores and releases bile into the small intestine.

See? Just as cool as the Avengers, right?

Poop: What's Normal?

Your poop can tell you so much about your digestion! I saw a survey on the news recently that said that 30% of people don't look at their poop in the toilet after they have a bowel movement. I totally get that it's no flower garden, but I think these people are crazy! Your poop tells such a great story—every time! It reminds you what you've been eating, how your digestion made you feel, and, best of all, helps you determine the condition of your gut. Your poop is the observable output of your mysterious black box (gut). By reading our poop, we can learn about our food choices and how our bodies have accepted them.

Remember what I said about shifting your schema? You need to start viewing your crap (literally) as something that can inform you on your health and help you know how to feel better. You see it at least once per day (or you should), so get to know it! Smile and wave if you need to!

There is no "golden standard" for poop (I mean, gold poop would be weird, right?), and everyone is very different. However, there is a range of normal characteristics of poop that indicate a healthy gut. By following these guidelines for healthy poop, you can use your poop to understand the condition your gut is in. Remember, I am no doctor and have not looked (nor will I ever look) at your poop. This is purely informational to help you understand your own digestion a little better.

Normal:

- Poop frequency of 1-3 times a day
- Free of pain or extreme strain
- The poop should be well-formed and easy to pass
- The color can vary significantly

Not Normal:

- Blood, mucus, or full food particles
- No poop smells like roses, but it shouldn't smell so bad that it knocks your socks off
- Frothy or greasy stool
- Painful or explosive
- Contains undigested food

Let's Talk More About Poop

The thing about poop is that there is not much to talk about when your digestive system is working in tip-top shape. For example, you don't hear people say "Man, my bowels are soooo regular!" Forget the fact that this is a taboo subject, people just don't talk about things when they are working. The phrase "talking shit" usually doesn't mean you're having an enlightening, tea-time conversation on the shape, shade, and size of your stool.

We've talked about how seventy million Americans have diagnosed digestive diseases[10]. Going further, did you know the National Institute of Health (NIH) has estimated that 9.8% of all deaths were a result of digestive diseases? Each year, there are two million years of combined life lost due to digestive diseases for people younger than seventy-five. What that means is that if you save all the lives lost from digestive problems, we would have two million more years of life for the collective population. The crazy thing is that we are just talking about people with diagnosed digestive diseases. What I'm trying to get across is that "poop problems" are serious health issues that more Americans have than they would care to admit. I'm guessing there are millions more that just deal with these problems behind closed doors—literally.

Think about it though—when was the last time "just deal with it" sounded like great health advice? Suppose you went to your doctor for migraines and she said "deal with it." Or your oncologist said "deal with it." Or your OB/GYN said "deal with it."

The gut doesn't have to be a victim of poor health. People chalk up gas/bloating, pain, and irregular bowel movements as a natural consequence of your food choices like, "That meal just didn't sit right with me."

Sure, that happens to everyone once in a while, but if it happens day in and day out, it's probably time to look at the greater problem.

I'll admit, digestive problems are easily tossed aside. It's really easy to blame it on something you ate and forget about it once you flush the toilet. Out of sight, out of mind, right? When nature calls again, you deal with it, flush the toilet, and forget again.

When I was pregnant, I heard lots of people talk about how terrifying constipation can be when you have your first postpartum poo. To be honest, there was way too much hype. The experience really wasn't that bad. So when I had some constipation issues that first week, I thought "Oh, this is just postpartum stuff."

The weird thing is that I continued to have constipation problems several times a week for several months after giving birth... and I thought nothing of it!! I would say "Oh, it's probably just postpartum stuff." It was brushed off time after time because, in my mind, it wasn't a problem. If somebody asked me "Do you have digestion problems?" I would have answered "No!" I didn't have problems with digestion, I was just constipated...

...wait... Isn't chronic constipation a digestion issue?

100%—Yes!

What I quickly realized was that my chronic digestive issue was NOT just something to be shrugged off. Rather, it was an indication of an underlying problem. It's so easy to just say "Oh, it's not a big deal." While many digestive issues can improve, you have to be willing to look into the clues within that pearly white cavern of your toilet. This "output," including how digestion feels day-to-day, is your biggest clue as to what's happening with your gut health.

Digestion and Bacteria

You might be wondering what this has to do with bacteria. Well, the bacteria inside your gut, your microbiome, influences digestion directly. From the moment you put food in your mouth, your digestive system kicks into a whole series of hormonal and chemical responses to aid digestion. When food enters your mouth, your mouth starts producing more saliva, which contains digestive enzymes to break down starches in that food. The stomach also creates bile and an enzyme to break down protein. The liver, pancreas, gallbladder, and small intestine also create fluids and enzymes to help break down food. Without all of these microscopic signal senders, we would not be able to access the nutritional content of our food.

This doesn't just happen by chance, though. Your organs don't just happen to have the biles and enzymes ready when you eat. All of these digestive responses happen because of hormones and neural reflexes. Think of it like a domino effect: one thing leads to another, and it will all run smoothly if it does. Digestion runs smoothly if it's in tip-top shape.

Can you guess who initiates those messages?

Yep, bacteria.

Many digestive hormones are produced both in the gut and from the gut cells, including gastrin, secretin, cholecystokinin (CCK), and gastric inhibitory polypeptide (GIP). To illustrate this point, one study looked at how the microbiome influences insulin production. When they inserted the microbiota of a normal individual into an individual with metabolic syndrome, they found that the person was able to become more insulin sensitive[11]. This implies that the bacteria in your gut has much more to do with digestion than we previously thought.

When the hormones and reflexes of the gut aren't functioning normally, all sorts of things can happen, from diarrhea, to bloating, to pain, etc. For example, the research is clear that people with Irritable Bowel Syndrome (IBS) have distinctly different microbes than healthy people[12]. This is true even for children with IBS[13]. So, distinct differences in microbes are reflective of the function of digestion.

Ever wonder how diarrhea happens? When the hormones responsible for muscle contractions "misfire," the muscles work out of order. Instead of gently massaging and pushing the food slowly through the intestines, the muscles chop and propel food and water straight through.

That's how you poop lettuce leaves, folks.

One of the biggest complications of digestive diseases happens when illness damages the small intestine. When this happens, your body literally cannot digest—or absorb—the food you consume.

Fact: There are 20,000 villus in each square inch of the small intestine. These villi are finger-like protrusions that are made up of absorptive cells. These cells renew daily and do all the absorption of your diet. They also help produce the enzymes needed to digest and absorb fats, water, vitamins, minerals, sugars, and proteins.

When the gut is inflamed, the villi are damaged and flattened. If you look at a digestive disease, like Celiac Disease, the symptoms can include diarrhea, gas, fatigue, anemia, and, in severe cases, bone loss and malnutrition, all because the gut is damaged enough to destroy its ability to absorb all the nutrients it needs.

Reap the Rewards of Your Food

Keeping the gut healthy is not just for people who have a diagnosable disease. Everybody deserves a gut that does what it's supposed to do. When you spend time and energy on fueling your body with healthy foods, you want to be able to reap the benefits. Think of it this way: Your diet is like the ingredients of the world's most perfect cookie. You can add exquisite chocolate chunks, the dairy's richest creamed butter, and organic, farm-fresh eggs. However, if you have an oven that's glitchy, the cookies aren't going to be well baked. Similarly, if your gut is not working optimally, your body will not get all of the benefits from your diet, no matter how well you eat. When your gut is working optimally, you feel great, digestion is free and easy, and your body gets the benefits it needs from your diet.

In the end, digestion is a delicate process affected by many variables, including those just mentioned. Little changes can add up to big results, particularly relating to how you feel. Being aware, informed, and attentive to your body's changes—even poop-based changes—can make all the difference.

Chapter Eight

Everything Is Connected

"If there's one thing to know about the human body; it's this: the human body has a ringmaster. This ringmaster controls your digestion, your immunity, your brain, your weight, your health and even your happiness. This ringmaster is the gut."
- Nancy S. Mure, PhD

The Disease Connection

While there is no magic bullet, I want to be absolutely clear that kefir is one of the best, least-known, practical remedies for creating a foundation of heath. It has everything to do with how we feel. Our gut is a central organ in our bodies and is connected to nearly all other bodily functions. Consequently, the choices we make about foods that keep our gut healthy are both crucial and overlooked. Cultured foods are an important element to a healthy diet, and a healthy diet is part of a healthy lifestyle. They all work together, like the parts of the car, to keep our bodies moving and aging gracefully.

The reason you should care about this research is because of what it's revealing about the cause of disease. There is a growing collection of scientific evidence documenting the connection between our guts and many of the major maladies of our time. Some of these illnesses include: obesity, diabetes, depression, anxiety, autoimmune disorders, autism, and the list goes on. Most interestingly, all of the diseases mentioned above aren't what most people would identify as being gut-related. And that's my point: to demonstrate that the gut is an overlooked pathway to relief from and help for an ever-increasing list of our world's most common ailments. Let's look at some the most surprising research:

The Second Brain

The gut contains over 500 million neurons that connect in a web-like structure along the gut tissues. This is the largest collection of nerves in the entire body, outside of the brain. In fact, that is why the gut is often referred to as the "second brain." Get this—the gut even has five times as many neurons as the spinal cord! So, when people talk about "gut feelings," it's more true than you think!

This concentration of nerves is called the Enteric Nervous System. Its primary responsibility is to regulate gut function via a large nerve we talked about before: the vagus nerve. The vagus nerve is a thick, dense nerve that runs along the back of your neck and communicates messages regarding hunger, pain, and even emotion. This system operates independent of the brain. The gut will still act on its own reflexes even when it can't send messages to the brain. That's why even brain-dead individuals have guts that still function. It works autonomously.

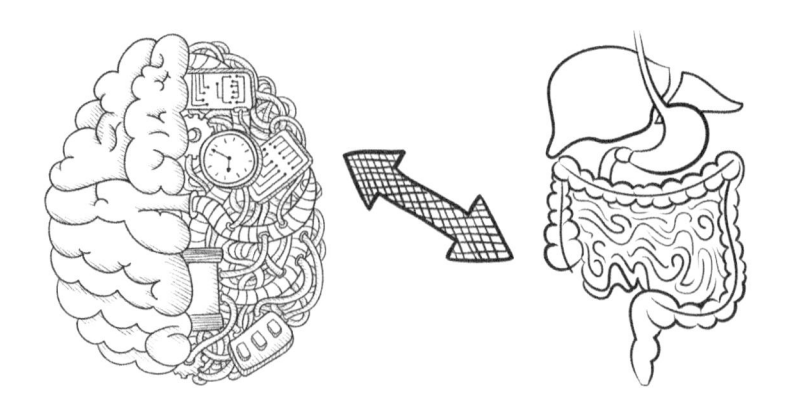

However, we were born with that connection to the brain for a very important reason: the nerves in your gut sense your every digestive need. The need for food (hunger) and the need to stop eating (satiation, or fullness) begin with a signal from the nerves in your gut that travels to your brain, which then brings the message to your consciousness.

There's even a formal term for this relationship, called the "Brain-Gut Axis," which simply refers to the interconnected nature of biochemical messages that transmit information from the gut to the brain[14]. These pathways give a scientific indication that there's a connection between gut bacteria and central nervous system disorders. Some even say that this may be a foundational piece of understanding neuropsychiatric disorders, including autism, depression, anxiety, and even stress[15].

Microbes and Immunity

Did you know that your gut is a major player in your immune system? There's a fact commonly seen floating around the internet that says, "80% of your immune system is in your gut." And this is mostly true. What this fact really means is that 70% of your active immune cells and 80% of your plasma cells (the things that produce antibodies) live in the gut[16]. Basically, these cells are constantly scanning for the presence of harmful pathogens. When they detect something, they signal a defense response. Any pathogen that enters the body through the mouth has to take on the gut's immune responses before it harms the body. Since we are constantly eating, drinking, and breathing, the immune system, therefore, is constantly active.

For many pathogens to do serious harm, they must pass the stomach—one of our body's primary defenses against outside invaders. The stomach contains gastric juices that are highly acidic, which kills most pathogens. Remember, the acidity in our stomach is strong enough to burn your skin, so this kills off most of the threats before they even get to the good part, your intestines. (I can hear you still wondering exactly how probiotic foods and supplements survive the voyage past the stomach; stay tuned for the upcoming kefir section).

For those intruders that do make it to the small intestine, they're met next with receptors called Payers Patches. The Payers Patches are the things that are constantly sampling the mucosal layer for intruders. When they catch wind of something foreign, they send out an army of white blood cells to wage war. The surrounding tissues also instigate an inflammatory response to buffer the action. They send off the messages needed for your body to start producing antibodies.

The cool thing is that gut microbes have pathogen-fighting capabilities as well. They act as allies to your body's lymphatic system. Like was just mentioned, inflammation is a natural response when the body is fighting to restore its natural balance. When you get a cut on your finger, the skin surrounding the cut gets a little red and puffy. This is inflammation. It would be normal to see this inflammation for a few days or even a few weeks. But we would not expect that inflammation to stay after the cut is completely healed, right?

This inflammatory response is good while the body is actively defending itself against harmful invaders, damaged cells, or irritants. However, prolonged periods of inflammation occur when the body starts attacking its own cells, or if that inflammation response doesn't turn off. This could mean inflammation lasting months, or even years. In the gut, chronic inflammation weakens the structure of the lining that separates the inside of the gut from the rest of your body. This inflammation is almost always present in gut diseases like IBD, IBS, Crohn's Disease, Celiac Disease, and more.

Having a healthy gut strengthened by the friendly and diverse probiotics found in kefir allows the immune system to focus only on those harmful invaders rather than constantly dealing with the barrage of damage that comes with inflammation. That way, the body is protecting itself instead of attacking itself.

Microbes and Autoimmune Disease

Over fifty million Americans are victims to debilitating, pain-suffering, misunderstood (and even more poorly treated) autoimmune diseases. Typical treatments include mega-doses of steroids, immune suppressive drugs, and antibiotics galore. There are so many questions about these diseases and very few answers.

The reason this comes up specifically in a book about kefir is because of the connection between the microbiome and the immune system. The gut is at the heart of immunity because of the vast immune responses that take place there. One of the key ways to manage and improve autoimmunity is to fix the condition of the gut. Fixing the gut reduces inflammation and heals the gut—both the physical lining and the gut functions. Fixing the gut and those essential immune cells inside helps the immune system do what it should instead of what it shouldn't.

Kefir, as a powerful probiotic, restores the bacteria of the gut. As was mentioned, the good bacteria act as allies to immunity, so proper restoration of the microbiome defends proper immunity. They go hand-in-hand. Not only does bacteria get in on the action by just being there, kefir specifically produces bioactive peptides that boost the immune system—making it more efficient. It has anti-inflammatory agents that reduce the T-cell response and also reduces the effect of inflammation and the damage of chronic inflammation.

Dr. Yuying Liu from the University of Texas Pediatrics and Gastroenterology department put it this way, "We know that gut microbiota are altered by stress, antibiotics, high-fat diet, and an overly clean environment. It is reasonable to postulate that lifestyle interventions could help to prevent or treat autoimmune diseases."

Microbes, Mood, and Behavior

Ever heard of those feel-good happy hormones you get after you work out or experience something pleasurable? They are called dopamine and serotonin. The microbes in your gut are responsible for 50% of your body's dopamine and a whopping 90% of your body's serotonin[17]. These mental health messengers are literally produced in your gut.

The interesting thing about dopamine and serotonin, though, is that there is an association between low levels of these hormones and depression[18]. When there is an interruption in production or transmission of these hormones to the brain, then our mood and behavior are affected. When this happens, the gut and brain don't connect as they should, and we feel different.

Remember that vagus nerve that runs from the gut to the brain? Well, there are studies being conducted right now using that nerve in treating depression[19]. Doctors performing a two-year study at Charité University in Berlin installed a pacemaker-like device near the vagus nerve to stimulate that nerve as if it were transmitting happy hormones to the brain. That way, the brain starts getting these previously dormant signals and starts getting those happy hormones. The crazy thing? it's actually working. People with an active vagus nerve and active dopamine and serotonin production were less depressed by the end of the study.

Scientists are also discovering that people with Autism Spectrum Disorder (ASD) have microbiomes that look different than most people. As a former teacher, this was particularly intriguing. It's commonly known that kids with ASD often have gastrointestinal (GI) issues, ranging from food sensitivities to chronic constipation and everything in between. On top of behavioral and sensory issues, studies have shown that, overall, those with ASD have an altered microbiome that is less diverse than normal. Specifically, they are lower in some healthy bacteria and higher in some bacteria like Clostridium and Desulfovibrio than you might find in the average gut[20]. Scientists are still trying to figure out the root of the GI issues. We don't know if the GI issues are a result of food sensory issues (and subsequent diet changes), or if they are a result of this altered microbiome—which may or may not be linked to ASD directly.

Looking at it from an interventionist perspective, some researchers have used probiotic treatments on mice that displayed autism-like behaviors, such as excessive grooming and vocalizations. These symptomatic subject mice were given diversifying probiotics. In a short period of time, this treatment reduced their autism-like behaviors[21]. This indicates that treating the microbiome may produce beneficial results for this and other social disorders. More research might indicate if this would be beneficial for kids and adults with ASD in treating both the severity of autistic behaviors and associated GI issues.

Diet, Appetite, and Cravings

Believe it or not, the microbes in your gut help regulate your appetite. These little bacterial messengers send hormones to the nerves, which then send messages to the brain, which then allows us to regulate our behavior. This includes hunger signals and satiation ("I'm full") messages.

Ever want to blame your cravings on something outside of your own will power? Well, researchers are hypothesizing that the microbes in our guts even have influence on our food preferences[22]. For example, seaweed is a common dietary staple in areas around the world. Americans on the other hand, eat little seaweed. Even if given the chance, I'm sure many would turn down the opportunity to try it. We Yankees usually prefer to eat foods without the word "weed" in the name (but we sure want to smoke it). Some countries, though, such as Japan, eat seaweed on a regular basis. What's interesting, is that scientists have found, in the microbiota of subjects from each country, bacterial indicators correlating with food preferences. Specifically, Americans don't even have the enzyme in their gut needed to break down the nutrients in seaweed, while Japanese people do. This could suggest that the genes and microbes in our guts send messages to our brain of the foods they want to eat.

Sound crazy?

Have you ever gone on a "sugar-free" kick? The first

time I tried it was during college. A few friends and I banded together to cut out processed sugar and foods with added sugars. We religiously read labels and ate things with no added sugars. We ate naturally sweet things like applesauce (no added sugar) when we wanted something sweet. If you've ever done anything like this, you know that those first few days are the absolute hardest. All you want is sugar. Your mouth waters when you see someone else putting chocolate in their mouth. But petty soon, I stopped craving it. It was like I no longer needed it.

The microbes in your gut demand the foods that they want to eat. If your gut is full of bad bacteria and yeasts, they want more sugars. If your gut is full of healthy bacteria, they demand more pre-biotics (healthy fibers). So when I stopped eating sugar, it stopped feeding the bad bacteria in my gut. I started to prefer things like veggies instead of candy and carbohydrates. I felt comfortable snacking on carrot sticks instead of chips. Sugars feed bad yeasts and bacteria, so they demand your body and brain to feed them sugar. Hence—sugar cravings.

Here's an interesting study that portrays this idea. Researchers used mice to study the effect of gut microbes on food habits[23]. They raised mice raised in a sterile environment, leading to mice with essentially sterile guts. They provided them with supplementary bacteria and then observed their food preferences. What they found was that these mice ended up developing more sweet taste receptors in their gut than they had prior to the introduction of the foreign bacteria. They preferred more sweets simply because their guts were different.

Likewise, another group of scientists also used mice to show another connection between our diet and gut microbes[24]. In this study, scientists basically destroyed the microbiome of mice in such a way that resulted in the mice developing a peanut allergy they didn't have before. During their tests, half of those mice were then given a special treatment that introduced a certain bacteria called Clostridia. This beneficial bacteria was able to prevent the development of a peanut allergy and kept those mice allergy free!

What all this research is saying is that there is a connection between the bacteria inside of us and the food preferences we have, our ability to break down the foods we eat, and our food tolerances (or intolerances). To date, there has not been a proven treatment in humans using this exact method, but these types of studies show that we're on to something important here! If this is something that interests you, stay tuned. The research is only starting to be released.

When it is fed something good for it, the gut tells the brain it wants more of that food in the future. One study showed that feeding the gut substantial amounts of prebiotics helps regulate a person's BMI[25] and can even contribute to a fuller feeling of satiation, leading to a regulated glucose response after a meal[26].

"Leaky Gut"—Is It Real?

Have you heard of this? Here's the idea behind the "Leaky Gut" theory: There is a wall of closely bound cells that make up your intestine's mucosa and submucosa layers. These layers provide protection against everything inside of your stomach and intestines, including food particles, acids, enzymes, and bacteria (both good and bad). It acts just like the skin, but on the inside of the body. When this layer becomes inflamed or unhealthy, the cells lose their cohesive integrity. This "intestinal permeability" allows anything on the inside of the gut to penetrate the mucosal layer and enter the bloodstream, hence the term "leaky." Any food particles, toxins, or good/bad bacteria all leak through the gut lining and into the body, where it doesn't belong.

The fact is, there is simply a lot we don't know about leaky gut. Right now, having a leaky gut is not a formal diagnosis recognized by the medical community. This theory is more or less a catch-all category for symptoms like food sensitivities, gas, intestinal pain, GI problems, and, to some, autoimmune diseases, thyroid problems, fatigue, weight gain, joint pain, and more. We know that intestinal permeability isn't good, but we can't say with surety that "X" leads to "Y" and that "Y" is that cause of "Z". With that being said, we do know that inflammation is damaging to the body. What's less clear is what the exact result of that inflammation is over an extended period of time. It's a theory that makes sense, but a theory none-the-less.

Furthermore, and most importantly to you, there is no single defined treatment for all of these symptoms at once. So if anyone tries to sell you an expensive supplement or magic pill for a leaky gut, watch out! There is no research behind any single treatment to cure leaky gut, as it's not even a diagnosable condition. Its purported symptoms, however, are very real for millions of people around the world. In the end, we understand the symptoms and the basics behind what may be causing them, but labeling any/all of these symptoms as leaky gut and taking a single pill or powder for their cure is nothing more than a scam currently making its way around the internet.

Chapter Nine

Sanitization Nation

"There's always a germ of truth in just about everything."
- Jim Lehrer

Grandma & Germs: The Invisible Threat

What's the difference between good and bad bacteria? The last few chapters were about the good bacteria in your gut—how having good bacteria benefits your health. But how many times throughout your life have you heard "germs are bad?" Did your high school health class ever talk about bacteria in a positive light? How many times have you shivered at the thought of touching something that could potentially be infested with "bad germs?"

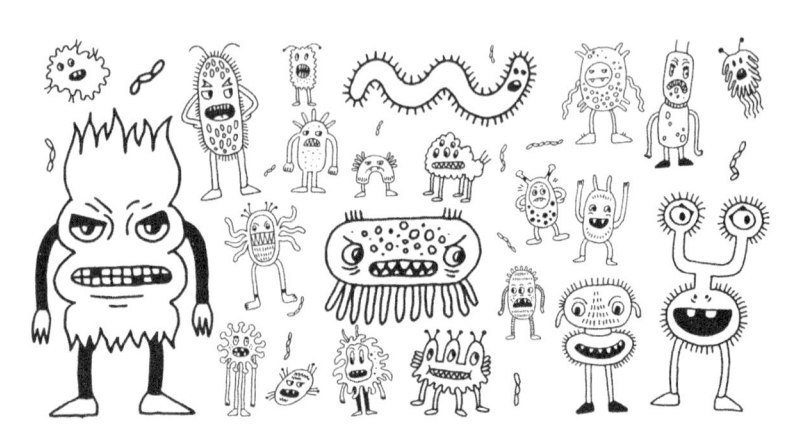

If I had to pinpoint any single person that believed that bacteria was evil, it would have to be my grandma. My grandmother's whole life revolved around bad germs. Although she came from an adventurous bloodline of hunters, fishers, and back-breaking farmers, she was also a serious germophobe. She was raised on a farm in the tiny town of Paris, Idaho. When we went to my grandparent's house as children, we always knew grandma's rules—always. They were some of my earliest memories! She was the type of grandma who scolded you more than she hugged and kissed you. Most of her rules revolved around being clean. To begin with, we knew to take our shoes off when we walked in the door. All children, after taking off their shoes, were sent straight to the bathroom to wash their hands before they touched anything or said hi to anyone. I spent more time washing my hands at my grandma's house than anything else I can remember. She never allowed a single pet in her house—ever—and kept all children (and men) out of her kitchen. She wiped her kitchen counters clean until the enamel of her 1970's countertops wore right off—literally. To this day, there are still visible circles scarred by the incessant scrubbing of those yellow vinyl countertops.

Growing up, my dad and his seven siblings were stripped of their work or play clothes before they even got into the house and were sent straight to the shower several times per day. She scrubbed them until their skin was raw and then scrubbed them some more. My grandmother was as devout to the "germs are bad" dogma as she was to anything else in her life. How did grandma get this way? Exposure to a lifetime of propaganda against the microscopic evils which are unseen, everywhere around us, and a fair amount of OCD.

Americans have been raised on the belief that germs are bad. We have been taught about this since we were young. Children even play games revolving around germs and "cooties." Throughout most of our lives we've been told, "Wash your hands! Germs are bad!" and "Don't share drinks, you'll catch someone's germs" or "We have to go to the doctor when germs make us sick."

Where did this phobia start? Pre-nineteenth century, several now-historically renowned scientists began to discover a connection between disease and microorganisms. Perhaps most famously, a French biologist by the name of Louis Pasteur participated in the formation of this idea called "germ theory" after he'd pioneered several experiments that ultimately proved the connection between unseen pathogens and disease. Pasteur, and others of the time, soon realized that many diseases were the result of poor hygiene, lack of sterilization, and the resulting advent and spread of bacteria.

Louis Pasteur

As the decades rolled on, learning from this pioneering theory, modern civilization began to adopt principals of sanitation and sterilization as a means by which disease could be prevented in both large and small populations. Workplaces changed, laws and codes were enacted, and parental attitudes gradually shifted to a general, albeit unspecific, awareness that mini, disease-causing monsters existed everywhere around us. And, the only known combatant against this unseen micro-army? Clean, clean, clean! Sterilize, disinfect, wash, cleanse, and purify! The general public didn't know exactly what it was they were cleaning against, they just knew that they needed to scrub everything. "Don't let it touch the floor!" and "Cook it till it's extra crispy!" were mantras to ensure the "little bad guys" were thoroughly dead.

Of course, hand washing and other simple sanitation techniques have saved millions of lives. There is no denying that. The leading causes of death in the year 1900 were pneumonia, tuberculosis, and diarrhea/enteritis. Today, it's things like heart disease and cancer[27]. While transmittable disease has taken a huge nose dive in developed countries, this is not true everywhere. Huge efforts are being led in underdeveloped countries to stop the mass spread of disease through simple sanitation techniques. We shouldn't go back on simple sanitation techniques that have saved millions of lives. Believe me—I wash my hands too, in case you were starting to doubt me. But what have we done with this message, that "germs are bad?" Have we, perhaps, taken it too far in some cases?

I'll tell you what we've done: we have sterilized the literal crap out of our nation.

Sanitization Nation

This "bad germ belief system" has become so engrained in us that it has reached every corner of our lives. In modern culture, killing germs is almost as necessary as breathing air. Think about how many of our daily habits revolve around sanitizing and keeping germs off our bodies. We wash our hands with soap and water after going to the bathroom and before we cook and eat. We use hand sanitizer when we can't access a sink. Our nation's schools are drowned in hand sanitizer. As a first grade teacher, I was given gallons and gallons of hand sanitizer every year from parents—literally. And every class used it like crazy! The classroom setting pales in comparison to medical professionals. If you take someone to, say, a hospital that sees many different patients, you could be looking at 100+ doses of sanitation per day!

That's just self-care. What about our food? Did you know that nearly everything you eat in the grocery store from produce to milk is sterilized? Even when we get home we continue to wash, rinse, and re-wash our produce again before we eat it. It doesn't stop there though. Did you know that the livestock we use for food in our country are given over twenty million gallons of antibiotics every year?[28] That's to say nothing of extensive pasteurization of dairy products, juices, all canned food, and produce.

My point is this: We have demonized germs and bacteria to the point that, ironically, it has become unhealthy. We thought all germs and bacteria were bad for us. But what if I told you that we actually don't have enough bacteria in our lives?

Think about all that bacteria in your microbiome. There is a lot of growing evidence that the lack of bacteria in our lives has led to new health issues. These modern health concerns have become national problems and are now as much on the table of discussion as transmittable diseases used to be.

I'm talking about autoimmune diseases and drug resistant bacteria. There are over 250 million people living with autoimmune diseases in our nation now. These are serious health dilemmas. Secondly, the overuse of antibiotics—those that kill almost all bacteria—has led to drug-resistant strains of bacteria that are non-treatable at this point. We have simply replaced old germs with new diseases and epidemics.

So, although we are living past some diseases that would have killed many of us a hundred years ago, the consequences shouldn't go unnoticed. We really are feeling the effect of it.

Germs Are (Mostly) Okay

Really! There is only a small fraction of bacteria that are actually harmful to humans. As hard as it is to believe, it's true. There is bacteria in and around almost everything you do. Bacteria doesn't just live on public bathroom toilet seats or shopping cart handles. It's everywhere around us. In nature, on our bodies, in our food, on nearly every surface we walk and touch. The simple fact is, unless you take a trip to outer space, you'll never truly escape it. However, the average person is not likely to get sick from touching most of it. Like I explained before, our bodies know what to do with bad bacteria. We can be exposed to many germs and not get sick. In fact, you have dozens of strains of bad bacteria and yeasts in your body right now that are not making you sick.

Healthy exposure to germs is totally okay—in fact, it can be a good thing. It's this exposure to germs that builds a child's immune system as they develop during childhood. We have an immune system for a reason. Even if, by chance, we do get sick, our immune system knows what to do in most cases.

So what's the difference between good bacteria and bad bacteria? Good bacteria benefits the hosts' health. It does this by promoting wellness in the body's natural ecosystem of bacteria that lives in and on you. Bad bacteria can make you sick, throws off the normal microflora, and can weaken the stomach lining. Bad bacteria can be found just about anywhere, but remember, it lives in your gut too. The normal ratio of good to bad bacteria is about 85:15. Both good and bad bacteria have a place in the world. It has always been, and will always be, this way.

Food with Bacteria

Hopefully, this knowledge about bacteria will make you a little less germophobic. If you need to put the book down to let this all soak in, now would be a great time (just don't set it on the floor—that would be gross).

I'm sure most people can talk about bacteria, in general, just fine, but how does it make you feel when we use the words "bacteria" and "food" in the same sentence? Absolutely squirmy, right? Let's try.

You go to a fancy few restaurant downtown. A waiter brings you out the delicious, juicy burger you ordered. He puts it right in front of you and says, "Dinner is served, with complimentary bacteria gathered and cultured straight from the chef's kitchen." You look up at the waiter, shocked, and do a double take back at your burger.

"No thanks," right?

Try this one: You go to your favorite grocery market to pick up some things for dinner. You stop by the deli and notice a new label on everything on the shelves: "Contains Bacteria." Instead of a normal food label, your mind creates a toxic hazardous symbol and you run from the store crying. Okay, maybe not crying, but running at least. (My grandma would've cried.)

That's why when I tell people about kefir they get absolutely freaked out. "You actually drink bacteria-infested milk?"

Why, yes. Yes, I do.

...And I like it.

Kefir is made when bacteria infiltrates milk with billions of probiotics. It is one of many foods in this "cultured food" category. Food cultured with bacteria is so foreign to most Americans. We have sanitized our food for so long that many people don't even know what cultured food is. I totally grew up in this category. I had never heard of it, never knew what probiotics were, and the only way I knew to "keep" food longer was by freezing it or canning it. My mom canned peaches and veggies from our garden every year, but again—canning is about heating foods to a temperature that kills all bacteria. It's at quite the opposite of cultured foods.

On a side note, canning does more than kill bacteria. One study reported that up to 50% of foods' vitamin C was lost during the blanching process[29]. Fermentation, on the other hand, never uses heat. It allows good bacteria to grow. That good bacteria is strong enough to overpower (and literally kill) harmful bacteria. It preserves, and even enhances, the nutrition.

In the thousands of years previous to today, people survived the changing seasons and preserved fresh foods solely by means of fermentation. You either ate your food right away, dried it (think dried fruit or jerky), or you fermented it. If you didn't use one of these methods, it just went bad. Refrigeration wasn't a thing yet. So when refrigeration did come around in 1854, everything changed. With the invention of the first commercial ice-making machine, grocery stores could store meats, produce, and dairy much longer than ever before. If you go to your local grocery store, nearly all fresh foods have been cooled and chilled in wait for our squeaky shopping cart to collect them. Many of your fruits and veggies are moistened and kept safely on the shelf. Your meats and cheeses all cooly wait for your picking. Without it, vegetables would be rotting, meat would be stinking, and dairy would go sour.

Fermented food, though, is the gut healing kind of food. The bacteria inside them contributes to the microflora inside our gut. Sterilized food, on the other hand, does not. Some even say that foods grown in your own garden and in your own, fresh soil have many more natural enzymes, as well as other associated benefits.

Antibiotics

Antibiotics are both a saving grace and a healing downfall. There is no denying they have saved millions of lives and are a modern medical miracle. However, antibiotic use has some pretty severe side effects. That Z-pack may make you feel fantastic, but it comes at a cost, both now and later on. Did you know that 30% of antibiotics prescribed in the US are not even needed?[30] That's almost one out of every three antibiotic prescriptions that don't even need to be prescribed. Further, the CDC reports that up to 50% of those prescribing or using antibiotics have misused them in terms of inappropriate selection, dosing, duration, etc.

The reason I call them a heath downfall is because they can be absolutely disastrous to our microbiome. If a person gets a bacterial infection, then antibiotics really do a great job killing off that bad bacteria inside. However, they also do a great job at killing off good bacteria. It's just collateral damage. Think of an empty field that is full of weeds. If you want to get rid of the weeds, you can burn them with a controlled fire. This will do a great job taking care of those weeds, but it will also kill everything else in the field. That's how antibiotics work. You will lose some of your good bacteria in your gut as well as the bad. While an antibiotic treatment takes you one step closer to healing your bacterial infection, they can also take your gut health one step back.

Because of this overuse, the bacteria that antibiotics are meant to kill are now becoming resistant to treatment. This happens by way of natural selection. There are always small amounts of bacteria that do not get killed during treatment.

This bacteria left behind then evolves to be able to survive the next time it encounters the same treatment. The bacteria that is not killed is left behind and continues to grow and flourish. For every course of antibiotic treatment, that bacteria becomes stronger. The alarming thing is, for many of these drug-resistant "super bugs," we have zero treatment options, even in today's modern world.

Those that take a course of antibiotics are more at risk for developing an antibiotic-resistant infection. That means they are becoming resistant for both you and I, alike. It's not a matter of who takes them, it's about the actual bacteria becoming resistant nationwide—even worldwide. This bacteria would resist treatment regardless of who is the host. The same CDC report mentioned above states that over two million people in the US fall victim to these infections. Sadly, this also results in more than 23,000 deaths per year.

This overuse is even worse when it comes to kids. Did you know that the average US child gets three courses of antibiotics before the age of two? The first few years of life are meant to be spent building and growing a diverse microbiome, so antibiotic treatments can negatively interfere with a child's growing and developing microbiome. In fact, one study even showed a correlation between antibiotic use before the age of two and higher rates of obesity[31].

Moderation, Wisdom, and Judgment

Again, I want to make it clear that I wholeheartedly believe in the principals of cleanliness, sanitation, and responsible use of antibiotics. These practices have been wonderful remedies, serving as blessings to the entire human race. Generally speaking, we're healthier and happier when we're clean and tidy. However, we need to refrain from painting with a broad brush and labeling all bacteria as bad, sickness-inducing, mini-monsters—because it's just not true. In the most literal sense, our lives depend upon bacteria. The sooner we're able to come to the understanding that our bodies were designed to be shared with our little microbe friends, the better. Maybe then we'll stop trying to drown out any and all unseen "microbial enemies" by bathing ourselves—and our children—in gallons of hand sanitizer, as if living in a completely sterile environment is somehow good for us. The fact of the matter is, unless you're having surgery and you're lying on the table with an open wound, living in a bacterial vacuum isn't healthy. Never has been, never will be.

Now, before you move on to Part 2, go rub some dirt on your fingers—it'll be good for you!

Part Two

This Is Kefir

Chapter Ten

The Kefir Story

"Out of difficulties grow miracles"
- Jean de la Buyere

"Miracle Grains"

When it comes to kefir, almost all research begins with a single name: Nikolai Blandov.

What's interesting about Nikolai is that he wasn't a scientist, a chemist, a doctor, or a royal dignitary; he was a simple farmer. He owned a dairy farm in the countryside of early 1900's Moscow, Russia. He milked cows for a living. His hands were symbols of the working class: leathered, muscular, callused, with a little bit of dirt found under each fingernail. His hair was dark, greying, and tattered, spending most of the time matted down beneath a simple canvas hat. His boots were worn and were more familiar with mud and muck than they ever were with clean cut grass. Nikolai was a simple man, a dairy craftsman of the early century, yet he helped unlock one of the greatest secrets Mother Nature has ever offered to mankind.

During Nikolai's middle aged years, rumors had begun to spread across Eastern Europe of certain "miracle grains" that offered health, prosperity, and vitality. Some even went so far as to equate these grains to gold in that, if one could acquire them, their life would be transformed both physically and financially. It's important to note that what exactly these "grains" were, what they did, and how they did it, remained somewhat of a mystery despite the spread of the rumors. Their existence was only made known to the general population by way of nomadic sheep famers, migrating from high in the Caucasus Mountains, near what is now the border of Russia and Georgia. Enigmatic though the stories were, their fame still spread rapidly, eventually making their way to Nikolai's ear.

Though Nikolai ran a successful dairy farm, producing a decent living for him and his family, early 1900's Russia hadn't been kind to him. His brother had recently passed away after contracting tuberculosis, and his parents had suffered for years, eventually passing away due to a debilitating case of typhoid fever. Appeals to the government by him, and others in the working class, had gone unanswered, and it was left to him and his fellow laborers to reconcile their personal needs by their own effort.

It was under these circumstances that whispers drifted

across the countryside of "miracle grains made of milk." Naturally, being a dairy farmer, Nikolai was intrigued and he began to ask around, gathering whatever information he could about what the grains where, where they were, and how to get his hands on some. What he learned was discouraging. With all of his inquiry, the best he could gather was that the grains were never given for money, rarely traded, and originated from a mountain range about 2,000 miles away from where he lived. Despite of all this, however, the deaths of his family members and his desire for health and prosperity led him to push further.

As the years passed, rumors regarding the grains continued to grow and began to shed more light on their existence. They came to be known as "The Grains of the Prophet," having been given as a gift from the Prophet Muhammed to nomadic shepherd tribes hundreds of years ago as a blessing of prosperity to the people. With the gift came a divine mandate to fiercely protect the grains (they were never to be given to tribal outsiders) or the miraculous healing powers would cease. As such, the grains became something of a divine oracle, only given to elder members of the tribe who had proven loyalty, faith, and dedication to tribal ideals.

Back along the countryside, however, things were becoming dire. With the recent advent of industrialization and the development of large, concentrated population bases, communicable diseases had become a plague of the new industrial working class. Working conditions were deplorable, and sickness spread quickly. Typhoid, tuberculosis, pneumonia, diphtheria, stomach diseases, and other ailments spread rapidly through factories and assembly lines.

It was amongst such conditions that rumors of the grains jumped from the working class up to the social elites of the time. When the all-Russian Physician's Society learned of the grains' existence, they knew they needed to obtain them.

Learning that a local dairy farmer by the name of Nikolai Blandov had become somewhat of a local expert on the grains, in a strange twist of fate, they reached out and enlisted his help to put together a team to search for and obtain the rumored grains, using whatever means necessary.

Nikolai, finding his long-time dream and passion now newly funded, set out with excitement to assemble a team, one member of which was his only surviving brother. They gathered several other men together, hired a mountain guide familiar with the Caucasus range, and boarded a train south toward the Georgian boarder. Once they had gone as far as the rails would take them, they gathered four donkeys and enough food to feed each of the men for two weeks, and set off up the rugged slopes of the Caucasus Range. The trip was planned to take about two weeks.

Eventually, they made their way to the village entrance. The air was thin, the wind blew strong, and the only sounds to be heard were the rustling of small metal bells attached to the necks of the scraggly mountain sheep who grazed the surrounding fields. The landscape, however, was breathtaking. There, high atop the mountains, hidden from the rest of society, a small pocket of homes, markets, and a church resting amongst the hills, untouched by the passage of time. At the entrance however, they found several guards, some on horseback, some bearing weapons, who adamantly denied them entrance to the village. Nikolai and his men had come prepared to negotiate, not engage in battle, and when aggressively blockaded out of the village, they had no choice but to start the long journey back down the mountain they had just climbed—empty handed.

Dejected, they arrived back in Moscow. For weeks, Nikolai endured the shame of failure in a country where money was scarce and the greater public largely knew that he had not accomplished what he had been sent to do on behalf of his people. Months later, Nikolai, seeing the sad state of the people around him, with the deaths of his family still fresh in his memory, decided to plead for the chance to try one more time. Surprisingly, his request was granted, but it came with the firm ultimatum that he was to either obtain the grains as promised, or lose all that he owned to pay the debts he had incurred at the state's expense.

Timidly, yet tenaciously, Nikolai accepted the terms and set out to try again, but with a different approach in mind. This time, rather than enlisting the help of his brother or other local village men, Nikolai headed back to his dairy. There, ankle deep in the mud, sitting on a stool milking the cows was one of his young employees, Irina Sakharova. Though she was a peasant and had spent her early life in hard labor, Irina was strikingly beautiful. Her hair was blonde and her skin was fair. Her blue eyes stood in contrast to the dark, dismal circumstances in which she worked. Nikolai approached her with a request for help. Having heard of the grains herself, Irina agreed.

A long journey and many weeks later, Nikolai, Irina, their guides, and a pack of misfit donkeys again approached the village gate. Once they were a few hundred yards from the village entrance, the group stopped. Seeing the guards in the distance, Nikolai reached into one of the donkey's packs and pulled out a large, worn yet imposing hunting knife and handed it to Irina. With the knife hidden beneath the folds of her dress, she approached the gate—alone. Arriving at the gate, she of course was met by the guards. Irina confidently, yet calmly, raised her chin and stated that she was there to see Bek Mirza Barchorov, the village prince. Seeing that the woman was very beautiful, alone, and appeared to pose no threat, she was admitted into the village and taken to the home of the prince.

As she walked through the village, Irina quietly took in her surroundings. The homes were small, made of stone, wood, and clay. Small windows adorned the sides, and smoke rose from within the walls of most buildings. Bustling about the worn grass were chickens, turkeys, pheasants, and other small birds. The village, though small, was very alive. She saw children running around, laughing, smiling, some hiding behind trees and giggling as she walked towards the home of the prince. She noticed small leather bags hung outside the doors of most homes. Each was worn and distended, and seemed to be full of some kind of liquid. The people there, with the exception of the guards, looked kind. Their skin was browned by the sun, with even the younger villagers showing wrinkles around their eyes from exposure to the elements. They appeared strong and their bodies robust from years of labor. Overall, the village seemed to be a pleasant place where the people loved to be.

Approaching the home of the Prince, Irina was introduced through a small wooden door and led to an inner chamber. Sunlight streamed through several high windows, a bit of dust in the air, as the Prince, Bee Mirza Barchoroz, entered the room. She quietly bowed, looked up, and straightforwardly stated why she had come. She had come having heard about certain miracle grains, that they offered health and vitality, and that people back in Moscow desperately needed them. The Prince stood there, listening until she had eventually finished explaining why she had come. He stood in silence and watched her. He looked at her hair and its golden hue, her fair, clean skin, and her tall frame. He admired the colors in her dress and the beads of the bracelet on her wrist. He had never seen a woman like Irina before. Taking a step forward, he reached out his hand and said that she was welcome to the grains, but that she could not take them from within the village. He asked her to stay, to live with him, and to become part of the village. He asked her to become his bride. Taken aback by the suddenness of the Prince's request, with guards watching from beyond the door, Irina quickly refused, and walked out of the house, lifting her dress as her brisk walk turned into a frantic run. In her frenzy, the knife dropped to the ground.

    The Prince, now embarrassed and infuriated, ordered men of the village to chase after and capture Irina. She had hardly made it to the village gate, just within sight of the watching Nikolai, when she was grabbed and ushered into a neighboring building. There was an audible fuss as people around the village gathered to see what was happening, and the gate to the village was closed. Nikolai, watching the scene unfold from a distance, knowing he had endangered the life of his young employee, gathered their belongings and rushed down the mountain as quickly as they could, not even stopping to sleep. Many days later, after arriving at the closest city, Nikolai explained what had happened and begged for help. The local police, familiar with stories of the troublesome mountain tribe, and knowing this was not the first abduction to occur, mounted a rescue force of many armed men who, with Nikolai, ascended the mountain yet again.

    Once more arriving at the gate of the city, this time surrounded by men armed with modern weapons, Nikolai demanded entrance to the village. Once inside, and having searched each home, they found Irina hidden away in a back room. Though she was terrified, she was in otherwise good condition, having suffered only a few scrapes from the scuffle. The Prince of the town was apprehended and taken to the court of the Tsar, Nicholas II. The Tsar, in exchange for allowing the Prince to escape a prison sentence and return to his village, was ordered to pay restitution for the kidnapping in the form of—you guessed it—the Prophet's Grains. The Prince reluctantly paid in full, delivering several of the leather bags Irina had earlier seen hanging outside the homes of the village.

Grains in hand, and with Irina at their side, Nikolai triumphantly returned to Moscow with quite the story to tell. Delivering the grains to the all-Russian Physician's Society, Nikolai's debt was forgiven, and he, along with his brother and Irina, were contracted to study and multiply the grains for the general use of the Russian people. The grains were put into full production and the first manufactured kefir was produced in 1908. The drink, catching on just as quickly as the rumors had spread, was distributed amongst the people. By the 1930's, full scale, industrial production of kefir was in full force. Kefir was now available to the masses, and all had access to the wealth of health that kefir offers.

Many decades later, Irina was formally recognized by the Soviet Union for her efforts and sacrifice in securing the grains from the mountain tribes. At the age of 85 she was awarded honorary status by the Soviet Union's Ministry of Food and Industry for her contribution to the health of the Russian people.

So, there you have it. From the tops of the mountains, to the top of your table, kefir has truly come a long way. And, just like the people of early 1900's Moscow, like Nikolai, you're probably wondering to yourself: What is kefir? What are these kefir grains? What do they do? Can they help me?

I'm glad you asked.

Chapter Eleven

What Is Kefir?

Let's Start with The Basics

There are two types of kefir: milk kefir and water kefir. The difference between the two is obvious—milk kefir is made with milk and water kefir is made with water. They are similar enough that almost everything I say about milk kefir is true for water kefir. Milk kefir is the default in this book, but there will be a chapter later for all the specifics about water kefir.

Kefir is a cultured dairy drink. The word "cultured" here, however, doesn't refer to some ostentatious, hobnobbed, cigar-smoking, fancy-schmancy person with a curled mustache. Cultured, when it comes to food and biology, refers to the growth of life—specifically bacteria—in a controlled space, such as a jar of milk. Kefir is created by placing tiny, white, squishy, bumpy bacteria starters (called kefir grains) into milk, and then allowing that milk to ferment over a period of time, usually around 24 hours. Fermentation is the process by which cultured foods work. The word "Fermentation" refers to the chemical activity of breaking down bacteria, yeasts, and other microorganisms in a process that usually creates heat and effervescence, which is identified by the tell-tale sign of bubbles and fizz. Those kefir grains are responsible for inoculating the milk with billions of healthy, thriving bacteria that help our guts. Once the kefir grains have fermented the milk, the grains are removed (strained) from the leftover liquid—a fresh batch of kefir!

Kefir
(with grains)

Kefir can be made from a variety of milk types, including cow milk, goat milk, sheep milk, and even coconut milk or soy milk (for the non-dairy folks out there).

When you place kefir grains in fresh milk, the bacteria and yeasts break down the sugars, or lactose, in the milk. The proteins and fats in the milk maintain their integrity, which means kefir is fermented, not rotten. That's a key difference. Similar to how grapes are safely turned into wine, milk is turned into kefir. This milk is not spoiled or curdled, and is a far cry from milk that has been left at the back of your fridge for too long. Kefir brings life to your milk by filling it with healthy bacteria.

The word kefir comes from the Russian word keyif, which means "feeling good."[32] Specifically, it's in reference to that "happy" feeling in your gut you get after you drink it. Because it's filled with healthy bacteria, it has the power to replenish your gut with existing bacteria, and then adds more strains of bacteria that weren't present before—like a probiotic ocean liner dropping off thousands of new, diverse, and exciting residents to the port of a city. It makes you feel great because it literally adds life to your gut.

Have you ever watered a wilting plant? It doesn't take long for that plant to perk right up and start growing again. That's very close to what kefir does for your gut. It brings new, rejuvenating life and leaves you feeling great.

What Does Kefir Taste Like?

Kefir has a creamy texture, a tart taste, and a slightly yeasty aroma. It's drinkable, but is thicker than the milk it's made with. When made correctly, it can have a slightly fizzy nature that creates a really dynamic drink. From fruity to savory, from drinks to cheese making, kefir is a very versatile food. It's a great base for smoothies or a replacement for things like sour cream or yogurt when cooking or baking, and it can be flavored in dozens of ways. Kefir can be one of the most uniquely delicious things to come out of your kitchen.

A Functional Food

A functional food promotes health and healing beyond the basic nutrition of that food. You'll hear these kinds of foods called functional foods, super foods, nutraceuticals, etc. More or less, these all mean the same thing.

Oatmeal, for example, is a functional food. Of course, oatmeal contains carbohydrates, protein, vitamins, and minerals like vitamin A and iron, just to name a few. But, on top of that basic nutrition, oatmeal is also a fantastic source of soluble fiber, which helps reduce cholesterol. This gives it the power to increase the condition of your health and decrease the chance of disease. Oatmeal gives you nutritional and functional benefits simultaneously.

Similarly, kefir is packed with nutrition because it is made with milk, yet packs a powerful, functional, probiotic punch with billions of little, friendly microbes. Of course, when you drink kefir you'll be getting all the nutrients from the milk, but it is actually made better because it has all of those newly grown good bacteria as a result of the fermentation process.

Speaking of nutrients, kefir contains the following:

> Potassium: Acts as an electrolyte by balancing fluids in the body (lessens the effect of sodium) and reduces blood pressure.

> Calcium: Builds and protects healthy bones and teeth. Helps with muscle contractions and blood clotting.

> Vitamin D: Helps your body absorb calcium and phosphorus.

Magnesium: Works alongside calcium as a chemical reaction with muscle contractions, blood clotting, and blood pressure.

Phosphorus: The second most abundant mineral in your body; aids in utilization of proteins, fats, and carbs for cell growth and energy.

Riboflavin (B2): Helps convert food into energy. Promotes healthy hair, skin, blood, and brain.

B12: Lowers the risk of heart disease. Assists in breaking down essential fatty acids and amino acids. Helps make red blood cells.

Kefir Nutrition Facts

Nutrition Fact #1

The nutritional qualities of milk are actually enhanced during the fermentation process. That means kefir contains more nutrients than the milk it's made with. For example, kefir has more calcium than milk. When kefir grains inoculate the milk, the bioactive products enhance this nutrient to make it more available to the body. This is true for B-vitamins as well—which are fundamental players in our body's function.

Nutrition Fact #2

Kefir has significantly lower amounts of cholesterol than the milk it's made with. Yup! The breakdown of cholesterol happens due to the bioactive acids produced by the kefir grains, meaning your body won't have to tackle the cholesterol itself. Kefir actually lowers the cholesterol naturally present in the milk. Kefir grains have this powerful effect through the fermentation process. Some studies performed on kefir show that fermentation can reduce cholesterol levels between 41%-84%![33] So, if a regular cup of cow's milk contains around 20 mg of cholesterol, then the kefir/fermentation process could reduce that amount to somewhere around 5-10 mg of cholesterol. Pretty amazing, right?

Nutritional Fact #3:

Kefir has fewer calories than the milk it's made with. You read that right—the bacteria from the kefir grains literally eat some of calories for you! And, because the lactose is consumed, this means your cup will have less sugar in it—meaning fewer calories. Measuring the calories, proteins, fats, and carbohydrates can be estimated by looking at the label of the milk you make your kefir with. You can estimate there will be a 20% reduction in calories and carbohydrates after the kefir grains have done their work.

The Kefir Paradox

Often, when I tell people what kefir is—a 100% natural whole food probiotic beverage—and tell them of its incredible health-promoting characteristics (digestion, metabolism, immunity, disease prevention), they get super excited.

"It sounds incredible!" they say. "How do I make it?"

I respond with, "Well, you start with a glass of milk, add the starter called a kefir grain, then let it sit on your kitchen countertop for about 24 hours."

Their response almost always results in a furrowed brow "...at room temperature?"

Believe me, I know that the idea of allowing milk to ferment on your countertop sounds gross. But stay with me here. This is where the kefir paradox begins to unfold.

Kefir Is Unnatural and Natural At The Same Time

Drinking milk at room temperature just sounds so unnatural. Like we already talked about, our brains have been trained to know that certain foods cannot be left out at room temperature—milk being one of them. You will hesitate with your first sip of kefir—just like I did—knowing in the back of your brain that it's "warm milk." However, on the contrary, kefir is as natural as you can get. Kefir grains were created by nature. Scientists have tried to recreate them in a lab and have never succeeded. These mysterious kefir grains naturally ferment the milk to create this probiotic in the form of a whole food. It is the antithesis of artificial and simply follows a natural process of cultured food creation. It adds life to your food in the form of healthy bacteria and yeasts.

Kefir Is Mysterious, Yet Surprisingly Supported By Research

I was baffled when I first came across kefir—perplexed that I hadn't heard of it before. I had never heard the name or noticed it in the grocery store. So when I caught wind of this gut-healing food, I was so intrigued. It also seems weird that I had never made cultured food in my own kitchen before. In a world full of information on everything under the sun, I found it surprisingly difficult to find anyone else who had even heard of kefir. This lack of knowledge in my social sphere led me online where, again, to my surprise, I found research article after research article, study after study, documenting the benefits and use cases for kefir and its cultured food companions. The highlights of those studies are found throughout this book. You can also find an ever-expanding list of them on my website, www.KefirLove.com.

Kefir Is Both Ancient and New

Kefir, believe it or not, has been around for thousands of years. It is generally believed that kefir grains originated in the Caucasus Mountains of southern Russia in the 1400's[34]. The grains have been passed down from generation to generation, and through their remarkable durability and ability to survive, they have left their microbial imprint all over the world. At the same time, if you had asked just about anyone in the US what kefir was 15 years ago, they would probably have no idea. Because of the recent literature on probiotics and gut health, kefir has resurfaced. Heck, we're in the midst of a full-blown probiotic renaissance! You see it on "Top 10 Health Foods" all the time on the internet, you may hear your friends asking around for probiotics, and you may even see it commercially produced and sold in grocery stores. It's definitely part of a cultured food revival that has spread awareness of making your own cultured foods in your own home.

Chapter Twelve

Kefir Grains 101

Kefir Grains—Not Actually A "Grain"

Many cultured foods like yogurt, sourdough, and kombucha begin with a starter culture that kick starts the fermentation process; kefir is no different. A starter culture is just a culture, or group, of bacteria that live together in a colony. Kefir's starter culture is called a kefir grain.

"Wait, so it's like, some type of wheat berry that you put in milk?"

Not quite.

That was my first image, too. Weirdly, it's not a "grain" at all. This starter culture has no wheat, rice, oats, cornmeal, barley, or any other grain in it. It's gluten free! Kefir grains are granules of polysaccharides (sugar structures), which gives them a firm, but squishy texture, kind of like a gummy bear. Inside this sugar structure is where the colony of healthy bacteria and yeast live. When the kefir grains are placed into milk, they start circulating these bacteria and yeasts throughout the milk, which kickstarts the fermentation process.

Kefir Grains

If I could go back in time and give this starter a new name, I would call it kefir hearts, instead of grains. This seems more fitting, because it is the life-giving force behind kefir. Kefir simply cannot be made without it. This starter circulates bacteria and yeast throughout the body of the milk, just like a heart circulates blood throughout our bodies. Without kefir grains, you have no kefir. It fills your cup of milk with life and goodness—it brings your milk to life.

It's helpful to think of the kefir grains like tea infusing your cup of hot water with herbs and antioxidants. Likewise, kefir grains infuse probiotics into the milk. In both tea and kefir, you take these things out before you drink the infused water or milk. Kefir grains are removed before drinking, just like a tea bag. The difference is that kefir grains are able to be used over and over again—you don't throw them out like you do the tea bag or tea leaves. Kefir grains are strained out of every batch of kefir and are placed right into the next batch. If they are taken care of, they can last a lifetime. If you make sourdough bread, then you know how that works. You continually feed the "mother" starter, and you can use it indefinitely to make rich sourdough bread.

Some grains are small like the size of rice, some are large, marble-sized balls, and some are even long and stringy. The small ones are generally new grains that are formed in each batch. Don't throw these out! They will grow in size if you give them enough time. Smaller kefir grains are actually stronger than larger ones. Because they provide more surface area to the milk, they are able to come in contact with more lactose, and, thus, consume it at a faster rate. If your kefir grains grow too large in size, they can simply be split into two by pulling them apart gently with your fingers.

When they're healthy and growing, your kefir grains should double in size about every two weeks[35]. Of course, this may not be true all of the time, but it's more of a general rule. Checking them between batches will help you monitor their size. When your grains grow too much, making your kefir ferment too quickly, it's time to give them away to friends. (Or store them for later in case your husband accidentally broils your primary grains in the oven at 450 degrees—true story). You can also throw them into a smoothie for an added boost of probiotics. Some people will even feed them to their dogs—dogs love kefir! Maybe they have a sixth sense about it being good for their gut...

Freezing the grains is technically okay, but I wouldn't recommend it. You may have success reviving them after storing them in the freezer, but I'll tell you that most of the time, kefir grains never quite regain full life after being frozen[36]. They never come back to full strength. So, if you can figure out how to preserve them without freezing, that would be the better option. Most people store them in a jar of fresh milk for 1-2 weeks in the refrigerator. Refrigeration slows down the fermentation process significantly, so the milk will only need to be changed after 1-2 weeks if the grains still need to be stored.

Inside a Kefir Grain

One really neat characteristic of kefir grains is that every person's grains are a little different. I'm talking about the microbial composition, or the literal content of bacteria inside the kefir grain. Since each is an independent colony living on its own and has spread from home to home across the world, different grains have evolved in different ways. People usually refer to them by their location, like Brazilian grains or Australian grains, but the characteristics of all varieties depend on their geographic origin, climate, and cultural differences. Their microbial composition is always going to be unique.

These differences only vary slightly, though. They all have the basic same bacterial strains. On average, the main bacterial strains found inside nearly every kefir grain are the lactic acid bacteria (LAB) strains: Lactobacillus, Lactococcus, Leuconostoc, and Streptococcus. Acetic acid bacteria (AAB) are typically always present in the form of Acetobacter. The yeast components include Kluyveromyces, Saccharomyces, Candida, and Torulaspora[37]. Say those ten times fast!

Kefir grains contain so much more than these, though, but I won't bore you with a complete list here. If you're curious and want to know all of the bacteria and yeast strains in kefir, visit my website at www.KefirLove.com.

A Symbiotic Relationship: Bacteria and Yeasts

Yeasts are similar to bacteria in the sense that they are in and around the world in which we live. These little single-celled organisms often live alongside bacteria and have a similar function. For example, when we use yeast in something like bread, it breaks down the sugars and turns it into ethanol and carbon dioxide. Sounds just like bacteria, right? Bacteria and yeasts are symbiotic, meaning they work, live, and thrive around each other.

There are millions of these cells inside your body and on your skin. While many of these yeasts are good and even beneficial for you, they are opportunistic in nature, too. If they grow out of control, it can lead to a yeast infection, like a vaginal yeast infection, oral thrush, or Candida overgrowth. This is what happens to when there is an imbalance in the relationship between bacteria and yeast. Remember that most of it is good, and it's good to include those beneficial yeasts inside our diet, too. The yeast found in kefir, for example, help with the production of short-chain fatty acids, which help metabolize our diets and reduce the risk of inflammatory diseases.

The bacteria and yeasts inside kefir are symbiotic. This means that they rely on each other. Unlike the major parties in the US political system, they co-exist. They are also interdependent during the fermentation process, meaning they are active and effective at different stages. This is another truly unique thing about kefir. Remember how I said scientists have never been able to recreate kefir grains in a lab? Well, they also isolated the kefir bacteria from the yeasts and found that the bacteria alone would not make kefir[38]. The yeasts alone would not make kefir. They HAVE to both in order to make real kefir.

Not all fermented foods have the yeast content that kefir does, nor do probiotic supplements you can purchase in pill form. The healthy yeasts found in kefir contribute much to the benefits that kefir provides. First and foremost, kefir works because the yeasts enhance the activity of the bacteria and vice versa. Of course, different strains of yeasts provide different effects, but they help with the production of short-chain fatty acids, improve symptoms of diarrhea, and have anti-inflammatory effects especially in your gut[39].

Sometimes if kefir grains are mishandled or mistreated (even if by accident), the balance of bacteria to yeast can get thrown off. You will know this is happening when your kefir doesn't turn out like it used to. Maybe your kefir was doing great, and then each batch got more runny and smelled more yeasty. This would indicate that the yeasts have outgrown the bacteria and they are no longer functioning symbiotically. Fixing that symbiotic nature is possible, so if this happens to you, be sure to check out the Quick Reference Guide.

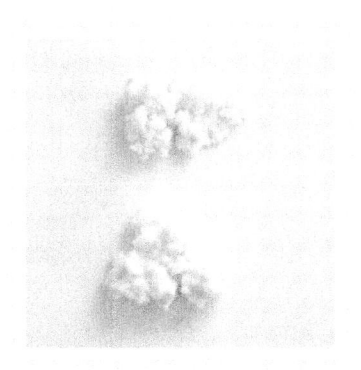

Dead Grains

Healthy Grains

Lactose

Because the grains are a living organism, they need to eat just like humans do. All that is needed to keep kefir grains alive is lactose. That's what they eat. Lactose is the carbohydrate, or sugar, in milk. The grains will slowly consume the lactose in milk over the 24-hour fermentation period. It's for this reason that kefir grains are placed immediately into fresh milk once a batch is finished. Without milk, they are like a fish out of water—a grain without lactose.

Lactose is a type of sugar called a disaccharide. This means that it's a combination of two different sugars: galactose and glucose. These sugars are found in all mammalian milks (like cow, goat, and sheep milk) and are a necessary component for a baby's nutrition because of its ease of absorption. Lactose is replicated for use in many infant formulas, and pharmaceutical companies use its unique absorption properties to deliver the benefits of their medications. Word on the street is that lactose is even used to dilute heroin to produce a faster effect. That's not the word on my street, but, you know, some other street... But don't visit that street!

Like all other living things, kefir grains also create a waste, or by-product resulting from their metabolism. If we eat, we poop, right? Lucky for us humans, the kefir grains' by-product has great benefits for us. Don't worry, it's nothing like our poop! When kefir grains consume the milk sugars, they release alcohols, ethanol, and CO_2 (which is the reason for kefir's fizzy nature). This is what gives kefir that distinct, tart flavor. All the sweet stuff is replaced.

Some of you may have a bad relationship with lactose, though. But kefir is great news for all you millions of Americans who are lactose-intolerant. There is an extremely low amount of lactose in kefir. Most people who suffer from the gas/bloating/diarrhea symptoms after dairy consumption do NOT experience these with kefir simply because most of the lactose is consumed through the fermentation process.[40] We'll get more into this later, but for now, ice cream lovers rejoice!

Kefiran

Kefiran is a sugar found inside kefir grains. It is a water soluble exopolysaccharide that is unique to kefir. It's basically a sugar structure that you can't find in any other food. It is produced from the bacteria Lactobacillus kefiranofaciens. It's made when one glucose molecule and one galactose molecule bond together. When this happens, it creates a gelatin-type structure. This is the thing that makes kefir thicker than the milk it's made from. Kefiran is not quite as strong as something like gelatin, but it's kind of like pectin that you would add to make your jams and puddings a bit thicker. Your kefir will never turn into a consistency like jello, but kefiran is the thickening agent that gives kefir that nice, thick, creamy texture.

Kefiran may be partly responsible for the unique health-promoting characteristics of kefir alone. Studies indicate that kefiran can have positive effects on lower blood pressure and cholesterol.[41] Other studies have indicated that it may have some kind of anti-inflammatory effect on mast cells (a type of white blood cell important in healing wounds and protecting against diseases).[42]

One thing can be certain, kefir would not be kefir without kefiran.

Recap

Here's what you need to know to take care of your kefir grains:

- Be gentle and use plastic over metal.

- Do <u>not</u> rinse the grains in water.

- Keep them away from other cultures (yogurts, kombucha, sourdough, etc.).

- Gently pull apart any grains that grow too large in size.

- For safe keeping, put them in the fridge in your typical amount of milk for 1-2 weeks.

Chapter Thirteen

How to Make Kefir

Tools of The Trade

Making kefir is ridiculously simple. Likewise, the tools needed are nothing special. There are no spectacular machines or ingredients, no heating or cooling. It's one of the easiest, most effective ferments you can make yourself.

You'll Need:

Jar with a Lid: Using glass is best for visibility and is the easiest to keep clean. I also recommend glass due to kefir's acidity, which has the potential to "leach" materials from many types of plastic. It is best to use some type of glass jar, like a mason jar or hermetic clamp-lid jar. The lid can be a regular screw-on lid, or you can find a jar with clamp-down lid. If you want, or need, to be extra resourceful, using a coffee filter as a cap with a rubber band is also a simple solution.

A Plastic Strainer: Use a plastic strainer with very fine, soft mesh. These type of strainers are easily found online or in cooking stores. Just make sure you don't have large holes in your strainer or else you'll lose some of the kefir grains down the sink. I find metal strainers to be damaging to the kefir grains if you have to stir the kefir as it strains.

A Spoon: Grab your favorite plastic or wooden spoon, folks. Keep it simple. Using a stainless steel spoon won't actually harm the grains, but I prefer using a rubber spatula or spoon to be as gentle on the grains as possible when I'm stirring the kefir through the strainer.

Other Fancy Items That Can Be Handy, But Aren't Required:

- Cheese cloth, coffee filter, or nut milk bag for yogurt or cheese-making.
- Sprouting lid for fantastic ventilation during fermentation.
- Funnel if you like to keep things neat and clean.
- Digital thermometer: I always use a small digital temperature gauge.
- Measuring cups and spoons can be helpful
- pH strips for when you're feeling extra scientific about the fermentation process.

How to make Kefir

1. Soak — place kefir grains in glass jar of milk

2. Wait — leave at room temp for 24 hours

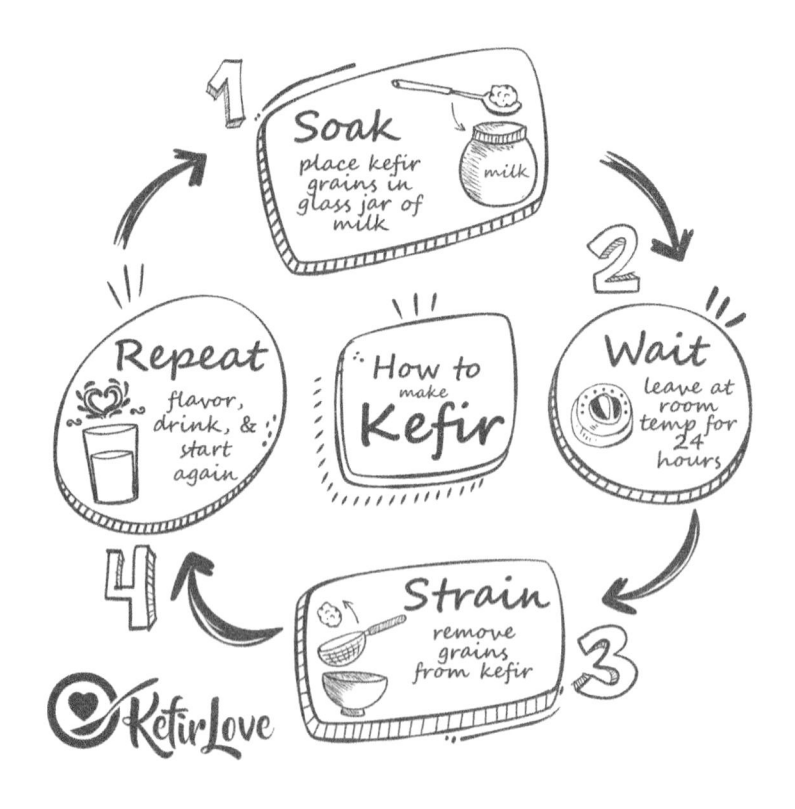

3. Strain — remove grains from kefir

4. Repeat — flavor, drink, & start again

KefirLove

Making Kefir: The Steps

1. Soak: Drop those kefir grains into your milk—just plop them right in! You will need about 1 tbsp of grains for every 2 cups of milk. For example, if you fill a quart-sized jar (4 cups), you will need about 2 tbsp of grains. This ratio of grains to milk will vary depending on your personal grains. Some grains are stronger than others, so you will need to adjust accordingly.

2. Wait: Leave the jar of kefir grains in milk on your countertop at room temperature for about 24 hours. Choose a place that is warm (72-78 degrees), but out of direct sunlight. In the warmer summer months, the fermentation can go a lot faster than 24 hours. It is okay

to move to the next step if your kefir is finished before you hit 24 hours. However, you don't want to leave grains longer than 48 hours. Once all the lactose is consumed inside your jar of milk, the grains don't have anything to feed on.

3. Strain: Use a fine mesh plastic strainer to remove the kefir grains from the newly made kefir. After the grains are removed, you now have consumable kefir! You can drink it right away or put it in the fridge for safe keeping until you're ready to drink it. Put the kefir grains in a fresh batch of milk to start the next ferment. <u>Do not rinse your kefir grains</u>. There is no need to rinse your kefir grains, and doing so washes away a healthy coating of bacteria and yeast that stays on the outside. That slimy white stuff on the outside is the kefiran, and it has a whole myriad of health benefits. That healthy coating on the kefir grain is key to kickstarting the next batch of kefir, which is important for keeping your bacteria and yeasts balanced.

4. Repeat: The kefir grains go back in the jar with some more fresh milk to start the next batch. If you start a new batch every 24 hours, then you have fresh kefir every 24 hours, too. The jar can be reused for several days before you wash it. Even if there is some residue on the inside, the kefir that sticks to the inside of the jar is full of those healthy bacteria and will help energize the next batch of fresh milk.

It's as simple as that—four easy steps! And, while you'll notice that the process itself isn't complicated, it will take some practice to dial in your results.

The Fermentation Process: Explained by A Nerd

It's a weird thing to be told to leave milk on your countertop for an entire day and night and for us just to trust that it's safe to consume. It certainly goes against our common sense. But when you understand the science behind what is happening inside that jar, you will feel a lot better! One scientist outlined the stages of fermentation specifically for kefir. I've translated the scientific language into layman's terms for your enjoyment—or in case you need a quick nap.[43]

> Nerd Language: "Inoculation of the kefir grains in milk begins with a grain:milk ratio of 1:30 to 1:50"
> Translation: Kefir grains are put in milk. About 1 Tbsp of grains per quart of milk
>
> Nerd Language: "Fermentation of the milk requires approximately 24 hours"
> Translation: Grains sit in milk for 24 hours.
>
> Nerd Language: "The homofermentative lactic acid Streptococci and Lactococcus bacteria consume lactose quickly and the pH drops"
> Translation: The bacteria in the milk starts digesting the lactose. The acids produced by bacteria makes the milk less acidic
>
> Nerd Language: "The low pH encourages the growth of yeasts and lactobacilli while it simultaneously causes the streptococci to decline"
> Translation: The yeasts kick into gear with at the now-optimal pH level, while more strains of good bacteria continue to grow

Nerd Language: "Yeasts within the kefir grains encourages the growth of heterofermentative Streptococci and begin producing lactic acid. Fermentation of bacteria are then favored over growth of yeasts as the fermentation continues"
Translation: As lactic acid is produced, yeasts slow down.

Nerd Language: "The yeasts synthesize complex B vitamins and hydrolyze milk proteins, using oxygen to produce CO2 and ethanol. This furthers the work of the LABs and inhibits the life and growth of bad bacteria"
Translation: Lactose is finally replaced with lactic acid, CO2, and ethanol. The bad bacteria are killed off

Kefir is one of the more straightforward cultured foods. Again, there are no fancy tools or devices, no extra steps or precautions. Just let the grains soak in milk, wait for 24 hours, then strain the grains out! The next section will describe just how to tell if your grains are working and help you master the art of kefir.

Chapter Fourteen

The Art of Perfect Kefir

The Artisanal Ferment

In kefir literature, home brewing is referred to as the "artisanal" method because it truly is an art form. The hardest part of learning how to make your own kefir is knowing what to expect—especially if you haven't made or tasted many fermented foods before. Everybody has a #kefirfail at some point, so be prepared to come back to this chapter when you need it.

Keeping in line with the paradoxical nature of kefir, while the steps to make it are simple, mastering the perfect kefir is anything but. Kefir is not quite as simple as making cookies—sorry. This isn't going to be a recipe with exact measurements and baking times with super predictable outcomes. Everyone makes it just a little bit different and unique to them. But why? Well, remember that we're working with living organisms here. Although science is happening, your crafting experience is quite personal. Two cups of milk for my kefir grains may not turn out like two cups of milk for your kefir grains. Your kitchen countertop and my kitchen countertop are different. We will use different milks and source our grains from different places. Our houses are likely kept at different temperatures—all factors that can affect the end product.

Although this seems like a challenge when you're beginning your kefir crafting, this can actually be a blessing. When you make it in your own home, you can adjust it to taste just how you like. By tweaking just a few things, you can make your kefir suitable to you. If you like a strong, tart drink, then you can ferment it longer. If you want it to be sweet and mild, then shorter ferments is the name of the game. You can flavor it thousands of ways for different occasions!

Be sure to check out the recipes section or visit www.KefirLove.com for more ideas on flavoring your kefir.

When You Need an Adjustment

Most of the time, adjusting one simple variable can make all the difference in creating the kefir you want. You'll find there is a sweet spot when you have the grains soaking in the milk for just the right amount of time—the kefir is perfect. It's tangy, but not too strong. It's smooth and creamy, but not runny. I definitely don't hit this with every batch, but when I get it just right, I can easily tell!

Below are the elements that play into how your kefir turns out. These are all simple fixes but have dramatic results. These are the levers you can pull, the buttons you can push, and the variables you can change when dialing in your kefir to goldilocks status. If any or all of these things don't help, then see the troubleshooting section.

Time

Time governs everything in kefir. You need to strain your kefir grains at just the right time before it over-ferments. You don't want to strain it too soon or the grains won't have time to do their work. The longer the time the kefir grains are in milk, the more it ferments. You want your kefir to be ready around the 24-hour mark at room temperature. This gives the grains adequate time for both the yeast and the bacteria to do their jobs. If you consistently cut the time short or let your kefir ferment for too long, it can create an imbalance in the bacteria and yeast relationship (and that can be tricky to fix). Again, aim for about a 24-hour ferment, but be willing to adjust the time if needed per batch.

Ratio

This is in reference to the ratio of grains to milk. How many grains go in how much milk? This has to be monitored or adjusted with each batch of kefir. It's a good idea to change the ratio when you need your kefir to slow down or speed up. Let's say you want to make an extra-large batch of kefir. To do that, you will need more grains to match the increased amount of milk—if you expect it to ferment in the same amount of time. Likewise, if your kefir is over-fermenting before that 24-hour mark, then it might be a good idea to change that ratio. If you take out some grains but keep the same amount of milk, then the kefir will take longer to ferment. I think it's best to start with how much kefir you want to produce. I like to make two cups of kefir every day for my family to drink fresh daily. So, I fill my jar with two cups of milk and then add the right amount of grains (which for me, is about a teaspoon) that will have the kefir ready in about 24 hours. Think of it this way: You want your kefir grains to have enough milk to consume as if they were running a marathon in your jar of milk. They can't finish their job if they're low on fuel, just like a runner can't finish a marathon after the body has depleted every ounce of energy. Also, remember that kefir grains reproduce and become larger in quantity over time, so don't forget to take some out when they grow too much!

Temperature

Kefir ferments best in temperatures 72-76 degrees Fahrenheit. Some people keep their houses much colder than this, which makes it a little difficult to get the desired consistency. Sometimes when you try to make kefir in colder climates, the taste will be "off," and it doesn't get as thick as you might hope. This means that it's simply not warm enough for the bacteria to grow. This is where that digital temperature gauge comes in handy. My kefir stays at an even 72-74 degrees during the summer months on my countertop. In the winter, I keep my kefir in my oven with the door cracked open and the oven light on. This is where I find my kefir does best in my house (as long as no one turns the oven on without looking first!). Finding just the right space that has an even temperature both day and night will help make the fermentation process predictable and will keep your grains happy!

By changing any one of these things, you should notice a significant difference in your kefir outcome. The only thing I will add is that kefir grains like consistency. They do best if they are treated the same every day. So play around with these things until you find something that works and then stick to it the best you can.

Signs You're Doing It Right

Kefir Smells and Looks Different than Milk

If you compare a glass of plain milk to a glass containing kefir grains, each sitting out for 24 hours, you will notice they are very different. Plain milk will be just as runny as before, and kefir will be thick. Plain milk will smell bland and possibly a little sour, while kefir will smell yeasty. This yeasty smell indicates that the bacteria and yeasts have been working.

The pH Level Will Drop

One of the key steps in the fermentation process is when the pH level actually drops, which helps good bacteria grow and bad bacteria die. You can actually order your own pH strips on Amazon for around $6. The final pH of kefir is around 4.1[44], while fresh milk has a pH around 6.6. You know the fermentation process is working if the pH drops.

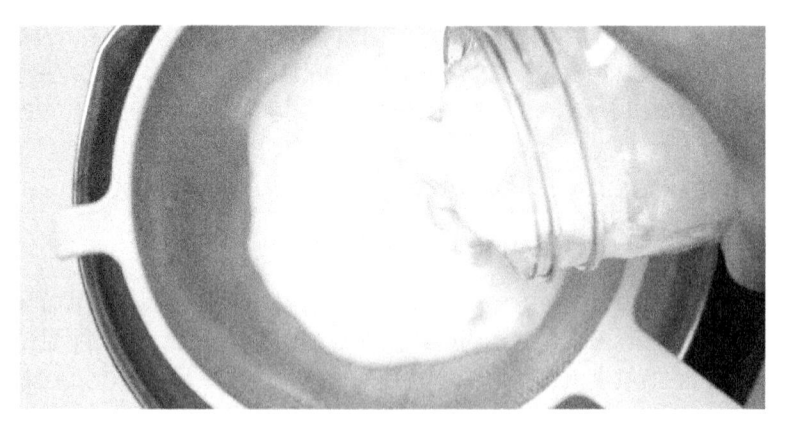

Kefir Will Start to Thicken

Remember when we talked about kefiran? This is the reason kefir thickens. It is infused into the milk through the kefir grains and acts as a thickening agent. This carbohydrate chain basically pulls together molecules to make them bond closer together, instead of leaving it in a more fluid form. Some have compared it to a pectin-type agent. Pectin is what is used in jams and jellies as a thickening agent. So instead of runny milk, you have a thicker, creamier kefir.

Bubbles!

After the bacteria has consumed sufficient amounts of lactose or sugar, they (just like any living organism) create another by-product called CO_2. That carbonation will be visible in your kefir jar as it ferments completely. The presence of CO_2 will appear in the form of tiny, carbonated milk bubbles. They start to collect at the top or bottom of the jar, or even on the sides of the jar. As the bubbles get bigger, they may even work their way up to the top of the jar, leaving tiny trails in the kefir. It won't look like a Coke straight from the tap, but you will see noticeable bubbles.

There Will Be Whey

Whey is the liquid protein inside dairy. Have you ever opened a container of yogurt or sour cream from the store and there was clear liquid floating on the top? That's the whey. When diary ferments, whey separates completely. So, you know your kefir is working when you see pockets of whey starting to form on the bottom of the jar or in little pockets on the side of the jar.

The Grains Will Float

Kefir grains will float to the top of the milk as it ferments. Healthy kefir grains start at the bottom and slowly make their way up. As the bacteria grows, they produce gas, which makes little bubbles inside the milk. These tiny bubbles help the grains rise to the top and float! Floating grains are an indicator of healthy, active kefir/grains.

How Do I Know If My Kefir Is Done?

Finding just the right balance for your milk kefir will be a delicate balance. This is the hardest thing to learn when it comes to making your own kefir. I like to think of it as checking on cookies in the oven. I start to monitor the kefir when I think it should be getting close, usually around that 24-hour mark. Just like with cookies, I look for those subtle hints that indicate "doneness," like the golden brown color of a chocolate chip cookie.

First, make sure that the kefiran has thickened the kefir

sufficiently. Do this by swirling the jar around in a gentle circle. If it's thick enough, the kefir should pull away from the side of the jar in a way that that is visible. It should stick together in one mass instead of running down the sides of the jar. It won't be like jello, and it doesn't stick to the jar like yogurt or pudding would. If you shake or tilt your jar, it should be obvious that the consistency has changed from its previous liquid milk state. This means that the yeast AND bacteria have both done their job. The kefir is most likely finished by this point or is a few hours away from completion.

The second sign to look for is the presence of whey separation. The goal is to strain your kefir before you see that separation. Once there are a few tiny pockets of whey separation, you know your kefir is done. The more the whey separates, the more fermented and the stronger your kefir will be. The more it separates, the chunkier and soupier your kefir will be (yes, I just said those words).

Over-Fermentation

Over Fermented Kefir

Hands down, the most common problem when making kefir is over-fermentation. This means the kefir grains were active for too long inoculating the milk. Kefir can also over-ferment easily when it is warmer than usual, which speeds up the process. You will know your kefir is over-fermented when you see the whey "pooling" on the bottom of the jar. The whey has separated completely from the kefir at that point. When you start to see an inch or more of clear liquid on the bottom of the jar, this is definitely over-fermented. Never fear though, this is not meant to be thrown out! If you accidentally let your kefir go a few extra hours and you have the separation of kefir and whey, it will still be 100% safe to drink! In fact, because it's been so active, there will be even more probiotics. Seeing this separation totally freaks people out, but remember that this is how cheese is made! What you are eating with cheese is the dairy that has all the whey squeezed or pressed out. When you see this in kefir, it just happens in a jar instead of a cheese cloth.

> Under-fermented: Runny and/or smells sweet, like milk. May smell slightly yeasty
>
> Kefir (just right): Thicker than milk, Smells tart and/or yeasty, Smooth (not too chunky), may see a few bubbles or tiny pockets of whey. When you swirl the jar, the kefir will swirl as a coagulated unit.
>
> Over-fermented: Strong smell. Lid may "pop" when unscrewed, releasing built-up CO2. Whey separated on bottom of jar. Can become runny, too.

Chapter Fifteen

Different Milk Types

What Kind Of Milk Should I Use?

The great thing about milk kefir is that you can use just about any kind of milk you want (with a few exceptions)! You don't need anything fancy or have to buy special products to go along with your kefir grains. They literally just need milk. You get to choose the milk that is best for your taste buds and for your pocketbook. That's part of what makes kefir so easy: anyone can get their hands on some kefir grains, grab their favorite milk and get those microbes growing.

Types of Milk:

Cow

This milk is readily available pretty much anywhere you go. Cow's milk is the most consumed milk in the United States. Any color of bottle cap will work; skim milk, 1%, 2% or whole milk. They all contain lactose! However, kefir is traditionally made with whole milk. The creaminess of whole milk really adds to the flavor and texture of kefir, especially since all the sugars are consumed during fermentation. I have yet to hear of someone who prefers a low-fat milk over whole milk in their kefir. Some people even say that the fat content in whole milk gives an added boost of health to the grains. Some even claim soaking their grains in heavy cream works well to boost their health and thickness of their kefir.

Goat

This is the second most common milk used for kefir. Goat's milk has a distinctive flavor that some people love and some people hate. Some goat milk products taste very "earthy" or "goaty," and some taste quite normal. There is a large variation in taste across different goat's milk products. This is due to the type of goat used for milking, their diet, processing procedures, and pasteurization differences. Goat's milk just doesn't yield the same consistency as cow's milk. One benefit of goat's milk, however, is that is has a composition of proteins:fats:carbohydrates that is most similar to a human mother's breast milk. It is digested very easily and is considered to be the "universal mother's milk." Other mammals are often fed goat's milk by caretakers when a mammal is not able to feed from its own mother's milk.

Sheep

This type of milk is probably the most rare, but it is accessible if you know where to look. Sheep's milk ranks highest in fats and proteins by far when compared to goat or cow. Because of the high fat content, sheep's milk is great for making cheese (more solid structures in the liquid). Interestingly enough, a true feta cheese is usually made with sheep's milk, or at least a combination of sheep's and goat's milk. Sheep's milk, too, is more easily digested than cow's milk.

Diary-Free Options

There are some great diary-free options for kefir-making, too! Don't get scared away too fast if you aren't a milk drinker. Diary-free options include using coconut milk or soy milk. You simply put your kefir grains in the milk alternative and let it ferment for your usual 24 hours. The grains may take some adjusting, so try it out a few days to decide how it's working. You can put the grains in coconut milk for about three days before they need to go back into milk with lactose—remember that milk kefir grains <u>must</u> have real milk to survive; it's non-negotiable. Milk kefir grains live solely on lactose found in all mammal milk. Give them at least 1-2 days of real milk before returning to a milk alternative. Also, use milk alternatives without any additives, as some additives may harm the culture of bacteria in the grains. For example, don't use vanilla-flavored soy milk—go for the unsweetened organic soy milk instead.

Keep in mind as well, when milk alternatives are cultured using kefir grains, the bacteria will grow much more slowly than cow's milk.[45] This means that the total bacteria count will not be as high as kefir with cow's milk. The growth of the actual grains themselves will also grow slower than normal.[46]

What Milk Labels Mean

Raw vs. Pasteurized: Both raw and pasteurized milk are okay to use with kefir. Raw milk already has lots of naturally occurring bacteria in it, so kefir will just enhance that and add more bacterial strains. It will also help ensure that any harmful bacteria that may be in the raw milk will be eliminated. The same goes for pasteurized milk. Kefir adds helpful bacteria and decreases any harmful bacteria that may be hanging out in the milk.

Homogenized vs Non-Homogenized: Homogenization is the process of breaking down fat particles. This makes it so the fat won't separate from the rest of the milk. Both versions are okay for making kefir and should produce similar products.

Organic vs. Grass-fed vs. Hormone-free: All of these are healthier options when you can get them. However, they are a bit more expensive than regular pasteurized milk. Getting the highest quality of milk is important for avoiding milk that has residual chemicals from treated cows, like hormones or antibiotics. Anything that a cow consumes will be passed through to the milk. As it pertains to kefir, though, all of these options are acceptable for making kefir.

Types of Milk to Avoid

The list of "types of milk to avoid" is actually quite short. Essentially, you don't want to put the kefir grains in ultra-pasteurized milk. Ultra-pasteurized milk is put through a process of high temperature heating—upwards of 200 degrees. It is more of a sterilizing treatment than a pasteurization. It can literally sit at room temperature for months without going bad. With this kind of shelf life and the denaturing process of high heat, it is not really suitable for kefir. Some bacteria might survive, but it won't culture. Some people who have done experiments with ultra-pasteurized milk and culturing yogurt say their yogurt never turned out. It ended up being a runny mess, rather than thick yogurt like normal. For some reason, many "organic" milks are ultra-pasteurized, so be sure to always read the labels before you buy milk for kefir making.

Chapter Sixteen

Water Kefir

Not Just for Milk

How can you get the benefits of kefir if you're on a diary-free diet? Two words: **Water Kefir**.

Water kefir is unique from milk kefir. It is much more palatable than most other fermented drinks, like kombucha or beet kvass, and is even more mild than milk kefir, which makes it a another great introductory cultured food. When you make it at home, it can be flavored just about any way you want! It's the unassuming, versatile probiotic drink that almost anyone can enjoy. It's like a healthy soda!

Water Kefir vs. Milk Kefir

Water kefir is distinct from milk kefir in several ways. Water kefir is exactly what it sounds like—kefir that is made with water instead of milk. So, naturally, it's dairy-free! Just like milk kefir, the bacteria consumes sugar and turns the drink into a glass full of healthy probiotics. However, since there is no lactose (milk sugars), water kefir must be made with sugar water or juice. The added sugar, or the presence of sugar, in the juice is what allows the fermentation process to ensue.

Water kefir also has more a distinct fizz than milk kefir due to the natural carbonation created during fermentation. That's why it's often described as a healthy soda. These fizzy bubbles are the byproduct of the bacteria processing the sugar. Just like with milk kefir, the sugars are consumed by bacteria and turned into carbon dioxide (amongst other things), which looks like hundreds of little bubbles inside your drink. The more fermented the kefir is, the more bubbly it will be.

The taste of water kefir and milk kefir are significantly different. Water kefir has a sweet, slightly fermented taste, while milk kefir has a stronger, tart, and creamy smack to it. The great thing about water kefir is that it allows for very creative flavoring. Sugar water is a blank canvas, so it can easily be used with fruity or herbal flavors and just about everything in between.

Water Kefir Grains

Water kefir is made with different grains that are unlike the "Symbiotic Culture Of Bacteria and Yeast" (affectionately shortened to scoby) that are used in milk kefir. Milk kefir grains cannot make water kefir, and water kefir grains cannot make milk kefir. They are two different cultures, just like sourdough and kombucha are different cultures. Water kefir grains are clear and crystal-like, while milk kefir grains are more bumpy and milky in texture. Although water kefir grains are clear, they can range between a crystal clear color to a brownish tint. This grain coloring varies based on what kind of water you use, the amount and type of mineral exposure, etc.

Another name for water kefir grains are tibicos, tibis, Japanese Sugar Crystals, California bees, or Ginger Beer Plant.

Like milk kefir, the exact origin of water kefir is unknown, but one theory is that the grains formed spontaneously on the pads of the Opuntia Cactus, in Mexico. It has been said that, traditionally, these crystals were gathered and used to ferment the juice of the desert cacti. While its origin stories center around Central America, water kefir can be found all over the world, and, just like milk kefir, every geographical location is a little unique in terms of bacterial diversity. Without historical records, we are just guessing on the origins, but we do know they have been around for hundreds of years. They are a symbiotic culture of bacteria and yeast inside a polysaccharide matrix, just like milk kefir grains. They, too, grow and multiply, and can only be sourced from other kefir grains.

In another difference from milk kefir grains, water kefir grains need minerals. If the water kefir or kefir grains seem to be lagging, stop growing, or slow their kefir production, then they may need more mineral exposure. This can be done by using water with minerals, such as spring water or well water, adding a tiny pinch of baking soda to a few of the ferments, or by adding some boiled egg shell (no egg, just the shell).

Are the Benefits the Same?

The biggest question I get about water kefir is: Does it have the same benefits as milk kefir?

Yes and no.

The benefits may be similar because they have similar bacteria, but water kefir has about 1/3 the probiotic diversity and potency of milk kefir. Water kefir only has about ten strains of bacteria. Also, both kinds of kefir have a few strains that are unique to each. For example, water kefir contains Lactobacillus halgardii, which gives it the clear color of the grain. It mainly consists of the Lactobacillus, Lactococcus, Lauconostoc and Acetobacter. Water kefir also has a handful of yeasts, maybe 2-4 strains, which are similar to milk kefir. So, if you're looking for a probiotic power bomb, it's not going to have quite the same healing power as milk kefir, but you do get some of the benefits. That's not to say it's not awesome, though! Water kefir still has way more probiotics than yogurt and many other fermented foods, and it still has those gut-healing probiotics, healthy yeasts, and organic acids that you're looking for in a healthy, homemade probiotic drink.

Water kefir is also said to be a great way to introduce fermented foods to kids. It's a fermented food, but the mild, slightly sweet flavors in water kefir make it an easy win for kids—and picky spouses. The only consideration to be mindful of is the alcohol content of water kefir. All fermented foods have some level of naturally occurring alcohol, but some say that water kefir seems to have a tendency to produce a bit more than milk kefir when you make it at home. Thus, mild, shorter-fermented water kefir would be best to serve to children. Also, keep in mind that fermenting fresh fruit or fruit juice is going to yield a much higher alcohol content than just sugar water.

Water Kefir

How It's Made

You'll need the same basic supplies as mentioned above for milk kefir.

1. Prepare Water: Boil 6 cups of water and add 1/4 cup organic cane sugar. The best type of sugar to use is organic cane sugar without any added fillers or anti-caking agents. Stir in the sugar until it is dissolved. Pour this mixture into a glass jar. Let the sugar water cool to room temperature.

2. Soak: Soak water kefir grains in sugar water for 24-48 hours. If you're using juice, just skip the first step and add the kefir grains directly into the juice. The ratio of kefir grains to liquid is about 3-4 tbsp of water kefir grains to 1 quart of liquid. The water kefir grains may stay at the bottom of the jar, or they may rise to the top; either is

normal. Water kefir grains do not need to be stirred or mixed during fermentation. It's at this stage that you may add dried fruit like a fig, apricot, crystallized ginger, or fresh citrus such as lemon or orange.

3. Wait: Wait 24-48 hours while the kefir grains ferment. The amount of time depends upon your individual grains and your personal preferences. A longer ferment will result in a more tart flavor and a higher alcohol content. A shorter ferment will result in a slightly sweet, more mild drink. In warm, summer months, the ferment may go faster, and in colder months, it may take longer. If you put fresh fruit in with the water kefir grains, then remove the fruit after 24 hours, and replace it with new fresh fruit if you're fermenting your kefir longer than 24 hours. Repeat this as many times as necessary.

4. Strain: Remove any added fruit. Strain kefir grains out through a fine mesh strainer. Put the kefir grains into the next sugar water batch at room temperature.

5. Flavor: Once the grains are removed, any flavor may be added! You can sweeten it with fruit, fresh juice, any kind of sweetener or syrup, or you can add it to any kind of tea or other liquid.

Special Considerations

If you want to make water kefir using coconut water or juice, this should only be done for a few days, after which the water kefir grains should go back to their normal routine of fermenting in sugar water. Returning them will keep the grains healthy and thriving so you get the best probiotic content, and your grains will be healthy and live longer.

A common question revolves around sweetening options. Like I mentioned, organic cane sugar is the best thing for the grains. Fruit juice and coconut water can be used periodically, but not for long periods of time. There is a short list of things that should <u>not</u> be used at all inside the water while the grains are in there: honey, maple syrup, coconut sugar, and molasses. These are all to be avoided in direct use with the grains. Of course, when the kefir grains are taken out of the water kefir, you can flavor it and sweeten it any way you want! This is for the sole purpose of keeping the grains healthy.

Some people don't go through the entire process of Step 1. They don't boil their sugar water, and that is totally fine. However, boiling water helps eliminate chlorine, should your water contain it. So, if you don't boil your water, be sure to use filtered water to keep your grains healthy and strong.

A second fermentation does the exact same thing for water kefir as it does for milk kefir. A second fermentation is when the grains are removed, and the kefir is left out for another 12-24 hour period. The bacteria found in the liquid will continue to grow and the fermentation process will continue. Many people are religious in giving their water kefir a second ferment because that's where the kefir becomes extra fizzy! If you seal your kefir in a tightly closed jar, the kefir will produce an amazing amount of carbonation, giving the kefir that fun fizz. After this, the kefir should be stored in the refrigerator.

Chapter Seventeen

The Benefits of Kefir

It's All About the Artisanal

Before we jump into all of the reasons why drinking kefir is good for you, I want to let you in on a little secret:

You may be aware that many grocery and convenience stores sell bottles of kefir—usually in the refrigerated section next to the yogurt. During my "kefir travels" I've talked to many people who say something like, "Oh, yeah! I love kefir! I buy a bottle of it every time I go to the store." Well folks, I'm glad you like kefir, but it's time to set the record straight. That kefir "stuff" you buy in bottles at the store is about 10% (or less) as effective as the stuff you make at home. It's watered down, diluted, and just plain weak when compared to the real deal: artisanal (homemade) kefir.

So, as you get started in reading about all of the wonderful, amazing, incredible benefits of kefir, please know that the bottled stuff you buy at the store just doesn't cut it when it comes to the benefits you're about to learn. If you're looking for health, healing, and genuine vitality offered by kefir and its associated probiotics, do yourself a favor and make it yourself. That's the stuff that matters. That's the stuff that truly makes a difference. That's the stuff that will change your life.

Digestion

The process of digestion (muscle contractions, enzyme secretion, chemical breakdown, etc.) is governed by hormones. Hormones, in case you're unfamiliar with them, are like mini chemical messengers—like your body's personal postal service—scurrying around delivering messages from one system to another. And, do you know what initiates some of that hormone production? Bacteria! In certain parts of your digestive system, bacteria signals the hormone production needed to get your food digested. Hormones kick off the muscle contractions, enzyme secretion, and chemical breakdown that makes it all possible.

Having plenty of good bacteria in your gut ensures that digestion can continue as it should. Looking into our microbiome's connection to digestion is especially important for people with digestive problems or diseases, such as Ulcerative Colitis, Crohn's Disease, Celiac disease, IBS, or reflux—to name a few. Kefir has a remarkable influence on the digestive system. Because it packs so much probiotic power, it helps protect the gut from the bad bacteria that can wreak havoc on our digestion. In one study, performed on hamsters, researchers were able to successfully prevent diarrhea in subject hamsters infected with C. Difficile, a pathogenic bacterium.[47]

More than just killing bad bacteria, kefir is also unique among other probiotics because it has the ability to re-colonize the gut—meaning, for example, it's able to re-populate your gut after a harsh round of antibiotics. The probiotics found in kefir are strong enough to land in the large intestine and take up space for a while, giving the good bacteria enough time to repopulate. Kefir, because it is milk-based, is able to buffer the pH of the stomach, once ingested, and thereby provide time for many of the bacteria to pass through to the upper intestine.[48] Most other probiotics are transient, meaning they only stay in the gut as long as the product is consumed. So, when you drink a glass of kefir, the gut has a greater chance of getting the benefits of healthy bacteria, killing off bad bacteria, and restoring gut health—a trifecta!

Remember the chapter on digestion? When bacteria and hormones are balanced and working properly, the intestinal muscles contract more effectively, giving you a much more pleasant digestive experience from start to finish.

Lactose Intolerance

The ability to comfortably digest lactose (a milk sugar) is a sore spot for 70+ million Americans who suffer from stomach aches, bloating, diarrhea, and even nausea after consuming any dairy product. There are two primary benefits when it comes to kefir and lactose.

First, kefir is 99% lactose-free. This is because any lactose found in the starting milk is consumed during the fermentation process. The sugars are converted into alcohols, organic acids, and gasses, leaving the milk lactose-free. This means kefir is suitable for even the most intolerant dairy sufferers.

Second, kefir has been shown to improve the overall condition of lactose intolerance. The kefir fermentation produces an active enzyme called B-galactosidase (lactase enzyme) that aids in the digestion of lactose. Studies have shown that this enzyme remains active in your body as a result of consuming it, thus improving your overall ability to consume lactose over time.[49] Some people have even claimed to cure their lactose intolerance completely through the consumption of kefir!

Reflux & Heartburn

For those suffering from reflux, GERD, heartburn, or ulcers, take heart—kefir offers something for you, too. In fact, kefir has been used to treat ulcers for hundreds of years in Russia. Even today, researchers are backing up the Russian tradition of treating ulcers with functional foods and modern medicine.[50] For those suffering with reflux or ulcers due to infections like H. pylori, one review of ten different studies, including over 900 people, showed that drinking kefir can reduce this particular overgrowth by 5%-15%.[51] This, as a result, can improve the condition of many digestive issues related to reflux.

Immunity

Remember when we talked about how 70% of your active immune cells and 80% of your plasma cells are found in your gut? It seems that kefir is also able to boost and support the natural functions of immunity already found there. This is because the bioactive peptides found in kefir are able to stimulate the immune system.[52] When kefir comes in contact with the gut, these peptides increase the gut mucosal immune response (IgA). One scientist also observed that kefiran (the thickening agent in kefir) helps balance the immune cells within your immune system, allowing them to operate as efficiently as possible.[53]

Lastly, kefir also acts as an anti-microbial agent—in that the good bacteria from kefir actively combat pathogenic (bad) bacteria. This means that kefir can even help prevent—and treat—an illness such as gastroenteritis.[54] So, not only does kefir help balance the microbes already in the gut, it also has the ability to overtake illness-causing pathogens it encounters along the way. The next time a stomach bug comes knocking on your door, you'll be thankful for the extra protection.

Autoimmunity

Kefir is an anti-inflammatory food, meaning it reduces the effects of agitation caused by the body's immune response. A diet rich in anti-inflammatory foods is critical for people fighting the effects of chronic inflammation.[55] One study demonstrated that kefir is capable of increasing the number of T-cells (a type of white blood cell), which is a key factor in reducing unnecessary inflammation. In one experiment, bacteria (lactobacilli) was isolated from kefir, studied, and was shown to both decrease the pro-inflammatory markers (things that cause inflammation) and increase anti-inflammatory markers (inflammation reducers).[56]

Further, as you may have seen in the news lately, rates of many allergic diseases are increasing at alarming rates, with diseases such as food allergies and asthma reaching all-time highs. What's interesting to note is that research has started to reveal a connection between our microbiome and the development of these allergy-based diseases. What we've found is that higher levels of certain bacterial strains have been associated with reduced chances of developing allergic diseases to begin with.[57]

For example, one study involving babies showed that infants who showed high levels of Bifidobacterium, L. acidophilus, L. delbrueckii, and L. helveticus had fewer food allergies and asthma later in life.[58] Two separate studies also confirmed that kefir and kefiran both have amplifying effects on the allergy reduction properties of these bacteria.[59] On top of this, another study performed on rats with asthmatic inflammation showed that kefir was able to decrease the inflammation enough to act as a therapeutic remedy and decrease symptoms.[60]

In fact, kefir is so well-recognized as an anti-inflammatory agent, scientists even used it to create a topical gel to treat skin burns.[61] Who knew?

Osteoporosis

You're probably aware of how important calcium is to building and maintaining strong bones. Measuring your bone density is important as you age because bone loss is a common problem if not prevented. As such, milk and other dairy products have been heroes in the war against osteoporosis for decades. So because kefir is milk-based, you may assume there are other bone benefits found in kefir—and you'd be right! One study involving forty osteoporosis patients showed that drinking kefir daily, along with taking a calcium bicarbonate supplement, significantly improved both bone density and bone absorption.[62] Talk about pro-bono benefits! (You didn't know dad jokes were included with this, did you?)

Cholesterol

High cholesterol is one of the primary, contributing factors to cardiovascular disease. Interestingly enough, kefir has the opposite effect on your arteries that it does on your bones (bones are meant to be strong, and veins are meant to be soft). This is due to the fact that kefir has a "softening" effect on the cholesterol within your body. One of the bacteria strains found in kefir is called Lactobacillus plantarum MA2. This strain has been tested in numerous animal studies and has been shown to lower total serum cholesterol levels, decrease LDL cholesterol, and reduce triglycerides in rats who were fed high cholesterol diets.[63] These scientists believe that the reason this happens because of a gene called the Niemann-Pick C1-like 1 (NPC1L1). This gene is critical in your body's ability to absorb cholesterol, and it was repeatedly present in this study. These studies further demonstrated that the rats had increased fecal cholesterol and bile acid secretion, suggesting that the cholesterol consumed in their diets was passed through their digestive system rather than being absorbed into their bodies. One study even linked kefiran to the ability to improve cholesterol and blood pressure levels.[64]

Antitumor/Cancer

Cancer, in its most basic definition, is the uncontrolled division of abnormal cells. It's a disease that starts with one tiny cell and grows to affect the entire body. It's commonly known that one key cancer prevention method is a healthy diet that includes plenty of fruits, vegetables, fish, healthy fats, calcium-rich foods, and fiber—just to name a few. What else is on the list? You guessed it: kefir. More specifically than just showing up on the list, though, kefir has the ability to stimulate the immune system to fight cancer cells and tumor growth:

> *The anti-carcinogenic role of fermented dairy products can be attributed, in general, to cancer prevention and the suppression of early-stage tumors, by the delaying of enzyme activities that convert pro-carcinogenic compounds to carcinogens, or by the activation of the immune system.*[65]

Several other animal and in vitro studies have shown that kefir can help with certain types of cancer prevention and early stage tumors. What this means is that kefir enhances the immune system at a cellular level, allowing the body to take charge and prevent the uncontrolled growth of what will become cancerous cells.[66] So not only is it part of a healthy diet, it also fits perfectly into the anti-cancer category as well.

Obesity/Weight Loss

Research has shown that obese individuals have an altered gut microbiome.[67] Specifically, they display a low diversity of healthy bacteria in their gut when compared to healthy weight individuals who, on average, present a much more diverse microbiome. Another clue to this gut-obesity connection is that, when an obese person receives a fecal transplant (it's a bacterial transplant really, but yeah, it's basically poop) from a healthy individual, their success in overcoming obesity is greatly increased. This tells us that gut microbiota restoration is a vital element in overcoming obesity.

These findings were supported by another study published by Nature: The International Journal of Science, in which human gut microbe samples were transferred to test rats.[68] The human donors included identical female twins, one of which had a normal BMI, while the other was considered to be obese. The microbes from each donor were transplanted to the gut microbiota of the separate subject rats of identical, normal weights. The remarkable result was that the rat who received the obese donor microbes gradually became obese itself, while the recipient rat of normal BMI microbes remained a normal weight. It was concluded that a tendency for disease perpetuation was present in the microbiota of diseased donors. And, while scientists admit they don't fully understand why or how it happens, we simply know that it does.

More than just assisting in bacterial restoration, kefir also helps when it comes to controlling those annoying cravings for unhealthy foods. The bacteria in your gut, whether they are good or bad, demand that they be fed (they are alive, after all). So healthy bacteria prefer to feed on healthy prebiotics in foods like veggies. Alternatively, bad bacteria and yeasts thrive on sugars and starches, thus demanding—craving—

their food through brain messages that sound more like a sweet tooth! Now, of course, these messages don't override your self-control, but having any support when it comes to changing your diet habits certainly helps!

Depression/Anxiety

As discussed earlier, the gut is connected to the brain and the greater nervous system via the vagus nerve. Because many of our emotional, feel-good hormones are produced in the gut, there is a connection between gut integrity and mental/emotional well-being. A broken down gut, on the other hand—one full of inflammation, poor structural integrity, and lacking microbiome conditions, is simply unable to efficiently communicate these hormones/emotions to the brain. Ask any psychiatrist out there: it's these broken down chemical-hormonal pathways that lay the foundation for depression, anxiety, and other mental/mood disorders.

Serotonin, specifically, is one such neuro-transmitter (brain messenger) commonly found to be lacking among clinically depressed individuals. Any guesses as to your body's home base for serotonin? You got it—the gut. The serotonin produced in our gut is also responsible for sleep and appetite. So, when the gut hormones are able to produce enough serotonin, we feel better. The probiotics produced in kefir help regulate these hormones. On top of that, kefir also produces a healthy dose of tryptophan, which is an important hormone in the nervous system—a relaxant that helps ease tense nerves.

Incredibly, one study even demonstrated that researchers were able to induce anxiety behavior in mice simply by altering their gut microbes. This confirms that central nervous system biochemistry is altered by gut inflammation—a damaged gut causes us to experience anxious behavior. At the same time, researchers were able to reverse the anxiety behavior by feeding the mice probiotic supplements, thus restoring gut harmony.[69]

Athlete Support

Ask any athlete you know and I'm sure they'll tell you: they pay special attention to their protein sources and intake. Protein aids muscle recovery and is the nutritional foundation of muscle growth. Kefir, being milk based, is, therefore, a complete, quality source of protein.

But the thing that makes kefir different from other complete proteins is that it is "partially digested" before you even drink it. When your body consumes any type of protein (a chicken breast, for example) it has to break down a chain of molecules into smaller bits prior to absorption; these "bits" are called peptides. These peptides have to be broken down further into amino acids in order to be digested. Ever heard of BCAA's? That's what we're talking about here—branched-chain amino acids. The smaller you break the protein down upon consumption, the easier it is for your body to absorb them. So, kefir is full of peptides (already partially digested by the bacteria), which means your body will only have one more step upon digestion to get those proteins into your muscles—and faster recovery means better performance.

This is why Russian weightlifter Dmitri Klokov, an Olympic silver medalist, drinks five liters of kefir daily in order to provide those proteins, nutrients, and probiotic benefits to his insanely large, muscular frame.

These benefits aren't just for weight lifters, however. Endurance athletes are notorious for having GI issues that interfere with their workouts. Exercise speeds up digestion, which is why the local gym bathroom is not necessarily the place you want to hang out. Studies have shown that long and strenuous exercise may alter the gut microbiota.[70] Probiotic treatments, then, help ease the effect of digestive dilemmas before, during, and after exercise.

Skin & Acne

This is one of kefir's hidden gems. Did you know that legend says Cleopatra (the ancient Egyptian ruler) bathed in fermented mare's milk and attributed her famously flawless skin to that practice? History tells us this was part of her beauty routine to keep her skin soft, nourished, and glowing. Although most benefits of kefir are made manifest on the inside, using kefir directly on your skin can be fantastic! Some have called the use of kefir on your skin and "anti-aging elixir," while others call it "weird and disgusting." The first time I used it on my skin, I whipped up a kefir face mask and left it on for an hour. As soon as I washed it off, I ran to my husband to tell him how fantastic it was! He had mixed emotions—weirded out that I just put kefir on my face, at the same time trying to be excited about something I was excited about. I now include a kefir face mask in my so called "beauty routine." I'm telling ya, it really works!

Before you run away laughing (or crying), hear me out. Kefir contains alpha hydroxy acid (AHA), which is a form of lactic acid that helps restore the pH of your skin. The beneficial bacteria is also highly cleansing and balances the cells in your dermal layer. What's even better, is that there have been some studies on acne. Acne, you say? That stubborn, embarrassing problem for teens and adults alike? Well, we know there is some connection between the microbiome and some skin conditions.[71] A 2008 study reported that patients with rosacea had a ten times greater chance of having a small intestine bacterial overgrowth (too much bad bacteria).[72] Further, some preliminary trials have shown promise for treating acne with probiotics. The idea is that the anti-inflammatory markers in probiotics could help reduce the inflammation problem in acne. The same goes for eczema, another inflammatory autoimmune skin condition. My inner 16-year-old self is rejoicing at the thought of it!

Women's Health

Guess what, ladies? You have a bonus bacterial ecosystem that men don't have! When scientists sample human bacteria, they'll take swabs of the mouth, nose, skin, digestive tract... and if you're a lady—the vagina. The vagina has its own ecosystem of bacteria that live, hang out, and do their thing separate from gut bacteria. It's called your vaginal flora—the unique composition of bacteria housed inside the vagina. That means that it comes with its own care regime if something goes wrong. Research shows that use of lactobacillus probiotics (such as those found in kefir) can prevent and treat the conditions of urinary tract infections and yeast infections—and that's by just consuming it normally, NOT a vaginal treatment.[73] One randomized placebo study on 64 women showed that consuming lactobacillus supplements during a yeast infection increased the chances of reducing symptoms by 37%.[74]

For all you mamas (or future mamas) out there, probiotic use before, during, and after pregnancy is safe and good for you, too! It's healthy for you and healthy for your baby. Remember, your baby's first exposure to bacteria will likely be your very own microbes. One study of over 200 women showed that probiotics during and after pregnancy can reduce eczema in their infants.[75] Women were given a probiotic supplement in the last two months of pregnancy and first two months of breastfeeding. Those infants had significantly less eczema than the others! Another study showed that women taking a probiotic supplement had higher immune markers in both the cord blood and breastmilk, which is great for fighting off disease.[76] In pregnancy alone, maternal probiotic supplementation has been shown to reduce glucose fasting levels, pre-eclampsia, and gestational diabetes.[77]

Too Good to Be True?

Now, we just ran through lots of studies, lab rats, and scientific lingo. It can be overwhelming, I know. But, stop for a moment and think about it. Did anything you just read stand out? Do you have personal experience with any of these pains, sicknesses, or diseases? Consider, just for a moment, that all of the benefits we just talked about, literally from your brain to your skin and everything in between, can come from a simple and unassuming glass of cultured milk (or water), that you made in a jar on your countertop.

"So, you're telling me this little cup of warm milk helps with all of that?"

Yes—that's exactly what I'm saying.

Chapter Eighteen

The Kefir Mystique

Yesterday, Today, and Forever

We started this section with a chapter called The Kefir Story about a man named Nikolai Blandov who, after several brave, Indiana Jones-like attempts, was able to secure a bag of kefir grains and thereby save the Russian people from modern pestilence. Now, I know we've been with each other now for nearly the entirety of the book, but would you lose all trust in me if I told you that story wasn't true?

To be honest, I'm not sure if it's true or not. In reality, that story is just one among countless others as to the history and origin of kefir grains. However, here's what we do know: kefir has been around as long as anyone can remember. Most accounts of its origin center somewhere in the Eastern Europe, particularly the Caucasus Mountains range dividing the countries of Georgia and Russia. Is that where it truly originated, or is that just the stage in history where people started writing things down? No one really knows. And that, my friends, is one of my favorite parts about kefir—its mystique!

In fact, if you look up the definition of the word "mystique" it's perfectly applicable to the origins of kefir:

> *"A fascinating aura of mystery, awe, and power surrounding someone or something."*

Isn't that great? That definition perfectly encapsulates the fascination mankind has had with kefir throughout the generations. On one hand, it's a legend passed on through the ages, its historical reputation always preceding it. On the other hand, it's as real and tangible as a common apple falling from the tree. We can see it, touch it, smell it, taste it, handle it in our fingers, etc. But, at the same time, we really have no idea where kefir comes from. It's that awe, that paradox, that sense of mystery that I love so much.

At the end of the day, the truth of the matter is, we just don't know for sure where it comes from, how we got it, or why we have it.

In that sense, kefir is kind of like Yoda—you know, that little green Jedi Master from Star Wars? I'm not a huge Star Wars geek, but I know enough to know that kefir and Yoda have a lot in common. For the five of you out there who haven't seen Star Wars, Yoda is an ancient master of "The Force"—an unseen energy or power that regulates and keeps the universe in balance. Of all the words used to describe Yoda, I think the most accurate adjective would be: wise. For me, if there was a symbolic embodiment of what kefir is, it would be Yoda. He's old, but no one really knows how old; he's been around forever, but no one knows where he came from; and he understands and brings balance to the unseen forces around us. I can just hear him now, "Drink kefir, you must. Good for your gut, it is."

The Stuff of Legend

So, in the spirt of the "kefir mystique" I'll share with you just a selection of my favorite kefir origin stories and I'll let you decide which one sounds most plausible.

Prophet Muhammed

This first tale is one for Hollywood, a slight variation of the kefir story from Chapter 10. This account begins with the Prophet Muhammed (born 570 A.D.). Centuries ago, Muhammed gifted the grains to Muslim tribes in the Caucasus Mountain region as a blessing of health and prosperity. He gave them the grains and instructions for how to make this health-sustaining beverage. The tribes were instructed to never give the kefir grains or methods for their production to non-believers, or else they would lose their magical powers. Rumor has it that these Muslim tribes voraciously guarded the grains' secrets, which were an indicator of wealth within their communities. The grains were passed down for centuries until early 1907 when a Russian doctor, Dr. Metchnikoff, published a book called The Prolongation of Life, highlighting his research on treating and preventing diseases like tuberculosis. As his work became more recognized and the possibility of a newfound source of health and healing became known, the all-Russian Physician's Society wanted to get their hands on the secret of kefir from these Muslim tribes. They quickly realized that walking in and requesting to buy the grains was not going to get the job done. So, they sent the Bandov brothers, successful businessmen and owners of the famous Moscow Dairy. And, as the story in Chapter 1 goes, the rest is history—or is it?

Manna from Heaven

Some say that the biblical "manna from heaven" was actually kefir. It was sent down from God to the Israelites who were traveling with Moses en route to their Holy Land of promise. The King James version of the Holy Bible describes it as "corn of heaven," while other versions call it "grain of heaven" or "food" or "bread of heaven." It rained on them daily and had, as the story is told, the ability to sustain their lives for the 40 years of travel. People claim that only kefir could be this "miraculous" and wholesome. Something this miraculous must have come from God.

Marco Polo

Marco Polo left very detailed records of his travels. He is believed to have sampled kefir in Asia when he wrote about his experience with a "pleasant milk drink." As far as his records indicate, however, he never took up the practice nor learned the methods of milk fermentation to take on the "road" with him.

Mother Theresa

Mother Theresa may have been given water kefir grains, also known as tibicos, from some generous Tibetan Buddhist monks. Reportedly, she used the grains and their healing effects to give to the poor to improve their health. However, she gave them only on the condition that they be shared for free, and were never to be purchased.

The People of the Caucasus

One thing that is agreed amongst most people is that kefir grains originated in the Caucasus Mountains of southern Russia. The Caucasus Mountains are a remarkable treasure. This high mountain range is located between the Black Sea and Caspian sea. Its highest elevation reaches an astounding 18,510 feet! This area is known for its particularly dynamic and well-aged people.

The people of this area are quite remarkable. It is considered to be one of the top locations in the world where people live long, healthy lives. The Caucasus range is called a "centenarian hot spot" where there is a high concentration of people that live past the age of 100 years old. We like to look at these kinds of people to study the aspects of their lives that contribute to their success in aging. Specifically, Abkhasia on the Caspian Sea has gained a lot of recognition and public attention.

One of the researchers studying this area, John Robbins, said that Abkhasia's diet, physical lifestyle, and cultural respect for age has much to do with their long success. Their nutrition comes mainly from plants and milk. It's estimated that milk and vegetables make up 70% of their daily diet, the rest coming from nuts, some whole grains, and very little meat.[78] Their food is often picked right before they eat it from their fields and gardens. When they do eat meat, the fat is cut off. Because they live on the steep mountain slopes, much of their life consists of walking up and down the mountains. They have no luxuries or cars and do all their manual labor necessities themselves.

Tradition in these high mountains tells us that milk was stored in a handmade bags made out of sheep stomachs. These bags were kept right outside the dwelling's door. It was customary to kick or punch the bag while going in and out of the house. The constant jostling would stir up the culture and milk and speed up the fermenting process. Culturing and storing the milk this way allowed the people to keep their milk longer without it spoiling, as refrigeration obviously wasn't an option. They would then pour out the cultured milk, consume it, and add more to the bag after they milked their animals, thus continuing the culture process.

Some scientists postulate that this is the most likely explanation for the origin of the kefir grain. They theorize that, within one of these sheep stomach bags, a perfect combination of bacteria from the milk and the gut flora of the sheep created a new, unique bacterial culture. Of course, we don't know for sure, because remember, scientists can't recreate them.

To these high mountain shepherds, milk is considered a sacred substance. Not only do they consume it every day, but it is believed to have a power beyond its basic nutrients. For example, sometimes a child in the community must be nursed and reared by another mother within the community. In this case, that child is considered to be a "milk sibling" to the children of the adoptive mother. Because the two separate children drank milk from the same mother, they now have a bond that is viewed more as blood relatives than any other relationship. Milk siblings are thus banned from marrying each other. Drinking milk is not only a part of their diet, but is also a fundamental, respected aspect of their culture and social life.

In the Abkhasia culture, old age is respected and revered. The elders are valued and honored for their wisdom and knowledge. One New York Times Reporter[79] traveled to Lerik, Azerbaijan and interviewed a man named Mr. Mavlov, who was 121 years old at the time. He reported having many children throughout his long life. One of his sons was 41 years old at the time, but, surprisingly, he also had a grandson that was 84 years old! Yes, an 84-year-old grandson!

In another account, reporter Michael Spector was speaking with the mayor of a city in the Caucasus Mountain area about longevity when he noticed an old woman walking down the road.

"Come over here a minute, would you? May I see your passport?" asked the village mayor. The woman took out a tattered, old Soviet Union document that listed her birth year as 1909, which, at the time, would have put her age at roughly 90 years old.

"Oh, take it back," the mayor said, abruptly returning the passport. "We don't need you. We're only looking for old people."

Back in the 1960s and 1970s, a lot of hype was built around the discovery of these centenarians. People were reporting themselves to be 168 years old! After further investigation, some of those claims were debunked, however, due to a lack of verifiable records. Still, many of the others were actually true and accurate, with several people living, verifiably, past 120 years old. Did you know that the average life expectancy of people in the United States today is somewhere around 78 years? And that's with all the benefits of modern medicine. It's truly remarkable that these centenarians are healthy, thriving, contributing members of their communities. One has to wonder what leads to such long lasting vitality.

In the 1970s, National Geographic sent Dr. Alexander Leaf of Harvard University and the Chief of Medical Services at Massachusetts General Hospital to investigate the Caucasus phenomenon further. Robbins describes his research like this:

> [We met]... a delightful trio of gentlemen who, like many elderly Abkhasians, were still working despite their advanced age. They were Markhti Tarkhil, whom [I] believed to be 104; Temur Tarba, who was apparently 100; and Tikhed Gunba, a mere youngster at 98. All were born locally. Temur said his father died at 110, his mother at 104, and an older brother just that year at 109. After a short exam, Leaf said that Temur's blood pressure was a youthful 120/84, and his pulse was regular at a rate of 69.
>
> The old fellows clowned around constantly, joking and teasing [me]. While [I] was checking pulses and blood pressures the other two would shake their heads in mock sadness at the one being examined, saying "Bad, very bad!" They never seemed to tire of friendly joking, always finding

new ways to have fun. [I] was impressed by their sharp minds, high spirits, and relentless sense of humor.

In the presence of such compelling accounts, you must ask yourself, "Could it be that kefir, and its associated benefits, have at least something to do with the amazing health and longevity of these peculiar people?"

I'll let you decide for yourself.

Chapter Nineteen

The Appetite for Things Natural

Artificial: Made or produced by human beings rather than occurring naturally, especially as a copy of something natural.

We live in a world full of artificial things. From clothing, to vehicles, to homes, to the internet—even our modern cellphone relationships—all of these modern creations are artificial, at least at some level. Have you ever wondered why this is?

I'll tell you why: Because human beings like to make things.

We create, we build, we produce. It's one of the fundamental components of our nature. We're all born into a natural world and, even at the youngest of ages, we desire to put our mark on things. For our early ancestors, that mark may have been something as simple as gathering mud together, forming it into the shape of a bowl, heating it by the fire, and having a container to store water in as a result. They wove ferns, leaves, and natural fibers together to create rope. They shaped bricks, stacked them together, and formed homes. They discovered various ores, melted them down, and conceived iron and eventually steel. The desire to invent was in their blood; it's in ours, too.

Somewhere in this human creative discovery process, the fabrication instinct made itself manifest in our food. Early on it may have started out as the simple roasting of a chicken over an open fire. Eventually someone found herbs, spices, and salts, and sprinkled them on the chicken and said, "Hey! It tastes better this way!" As the years passed we began to farm and industrialize. Instead of a few chickens pecking around a gated patch of grass, we realized we could scale their birthing process and farm thousands of them at the same time.

As the human population continued to grow and evolve, so too, did our inclination to innovate. The industrial revolution brought assembly lines, factories, and economies of scale to the production of our food. Eventually, the answer to the question, "What kind of bread is that?" changed from, "Wheat—I made it myself" to "Wonder bread." As our population further increased, and our living quarters became more dense, the production of food was centralized into large, industrial, commercial hubs that would then distribute to a local convenience store. So, instead of having to birth, feed, raise, and slaughter the cow, we simply pick up the four-pack of burger patties and swipe our card.

Fast forward to today and we find our modern-day grocery stores full of foods that have been far removed from their natural state. In fact, if you're like me, you pick up something like a package of Oreos and wonder what kind of sorcery was used to create such a delightful, yet obviously processed, "food" that seems to have no basis in any natural substance found on this planet.

"How the hell do they make these things…?" I wonder, slowly turning my head to one side as—I'm sure—other shoppers are wondering why I'm staring at a package of Oreos like it's a calculus equation.

The fact of the matter is, if you were to walk into your

average grocery store, 80-90% of those foods have been processed past any recognition of natural substances. Heck, you need a PhD in biopharmaceutical linguistics just to make out the ingredient lists. We went from "cooking chicken over the fire with a little salt" to "artificial growth hormones, injected into mechanically separated meat, formed into shapes resembling characters from Sesame Street, nuked in the microwave for 60 seconds." My inner 4-year-old is salivating just thinking about it.

Truly, the evolution of human food is something to behold.

Antithesis to Artificial

Natural: Existing in or caused by nature; not man made or caused by humankind.

I don't know if you've noticed, but we've recently seen a relatively abrupt counter-culture rebellion against the processed food world—the rise of the natural foodie. In a world dominated by the Walmart imperium, the Whole Foods rebellion arose, its band of hipster pupils in tow.

Suddenly, natural is cool again.

As a society, we're beginning to tire of fake food, or at least we're becoming educated enough to see it for what it really is: unhealthy. Whether it was the advent of the internet, food blogs, mommy culture, or simply the continued evolution of our preferences as human beings, we're developing an appetite for natural things.

McDonald's now offers milk instead of soda in its Happy Meals. Food packages advertise the simplicity of their ingredient lists rather than their tastes or conveniences. "All Natural" may very well be the #1 nutritional buzz word of the past 2 decades. We're worried about carcinogens and cancer. We flock to naturally sourced products. We abhor pesticides and cherish all things organic. We're starting to like a little dirt on our veggies—it's like we trust them more if our carrots look like they just fell off the farm truck. Commercials are full of images of rugged looking farmers plucking fresh fruit right off the tree and placing it directly onto our countertop. And, regardless of how accurate all of these packages, portrayals, and profiteers are, they're all doing the same thing: playing on our newfound appetite for things natural.

It could rightly be said that kefir is the antithesis to artificial. There is literally nothing about kefir that is man-made. It's as natural as the air we breathe, the salt in the ocean, and the rocks of the mountains. To our knowledge, it has existed forever in its current state. The kefir grains you use today look, feel, and perform in the exact same manner as the earliest known kefir grains used thousands of years ago. Kefir is the very definition of timeless. And how, you may ask, does kefir remain so unchanged throughout the passage of time? Well, the answer is that it seems almost divinely resistant to manipulation by the hands of man. No matter how hard we try to alter it (and believe me, we've tried), kefir simply remains constant in an almost eternal state. It's almost as if it's immune to processing. We poke it, prod it, slice it, dice it, break it down, tear it apart—and yet it endures.

For years scientists have repeatedly tried to recreate artificial versions of kefir in a lab. They attempt this by breaking kefir down into its component parts, bacteria, yeasts, etc., and then they seek to reconstruct these pieces into a new probiotic compound. And you know what, they failed—every single time. Never once has kefir successfully been recreated in a lab. All of these attempts at probiotic synthesis have yielded nothing more than dead bacteria and smelly yeast. In a world where it seems that everything is compounded, amalgamated, processed, or synthetically produced (in your face, Easy Cheese!), kefir stands timeless in its original, unadulterated state.

It's this eternally organic attribute of kefir that so completely satisfies our appetite for things natural. In this sense, it truly is the ultimate natural food. There's something so miraculous about it that it can't be formulated or calculated or manufactured, even if we wanted to. Whatever "it" is, I believe it's the same reason that this unique culture has thrived for centuries, passed down from generation to generation.

Beyond the fact that kefir is a pure, organic, natural artifact, is the reality that its sole purpose for existence is to act as an impetus for the kinds of bacteria that support and empower human life. In that sense, it could be seen as the ultimate sidekick to humankind's quest for wellness and health. Ask anyone who has experienced the effects of dysbiosis and they'll tell you, life without a properly functioning population of gut microbiota is no fun—it's downright miserable. Kefir seems to exist solely for the purpose of helping mankind feel better and be healthy, and does so in an absolutely, 100% natural manner.

Personally, I view kefir, literally, as a gift from God. This is a viewpoint that I know I share with millions of others, both historically and contemporarily. Kefir, though it looks like just a simple, little milk-fermenting buddy, seems to have been given to us to keep us healthy—to make us feel better.

The World's Greatest Natural Probiotic

People are drawn to kefir because it's one of the richest probiotics you can get your hands on. Sometimes kefir is called a "drinkable yogurt." However, comparing yogurt to kefir is just a bit unfair. It's like comparing my swimming ability to

Michael Phelps. Sure, I can swim a few laps, but I don't have 23 Olympic gold medals—catch my drift? While it's true that many yogurts do have probiotics in them—which are healthy, don't get me wrong—kefir contains hundreds of billions more. Did you know that you would have to eat about 10 cups of a regular yogurt to get the same amount of probiotic punch found in a single cup of kefir? One of my first encounters with kefir was a pre-made "kefir drink" purchased at a health food store. I was impressed by the label that read clearly and proudly on the front: "1 Billion!"

"Wow," I thought, "1 billion probiotics!"

Soon after, however, I realized that one billion, actually, wasn't that much, at least in probiotic terms. When it comes to probiotic effectiveness, one billion is actually pretty weak sauce. The recommended dose for a probiotic to be effective is 10 billion CFU—at a minimum! So, basically, this kefir drink I bought packed the same amount of punch as your average cup of standard yogurt.

I soon realized that, even though you can find bottled versions of kefir in your local grocery store, their power and potency are severely "watered down" when compared to kefir made at home. The reason for this is that it's simply not possible or practical to produce, bottle, store, and ship a highly active probiotic beverage due to the simple fact that, once a ferment has started, you can never really "turn it off." What this means for commercial kefir makers is that, if they distributed truly vibrant, living, potent bottles of kefir, the sheer carbonation created by shipping such a drink would cause bottle caps to explode just a short time after leaving their production facility. High-powered probiotics just aren't stable enough for plastic bottles being shipped around the world. So, in order to meet the demands of distribution, these "kefir drinks" are often dialed down to a much more dormant state.

In contrast, homemade kefir can contain hundreds of billions of probiotics per cup. When you make kefir fresh at home, the all of the cultures go directly into your gut. They don't sit while it gets packaged, shipped, or shelved. The probiotics are growing and thriving at the very moment you consume them—fresh. Did you know this is why many cultured foods don't label their CFUs in store products? Companies can't guarantee a bacterial count because they don't know how long their product is going to sit on the shelf before it gets to your mouth.

Another reason people are drawn to kefir is because kefir can have up to 56 different strains of probiotics. To help you get a better picture of what this means, yogurt has around 2-5 strains and kombucha has somewhere around ten. On top of that, I have never seen a probiotic supplement with more than a handful of different strains. You may be thinking, "Big deal, bacteria is bacteria, right?" Well, remember that your body has a thousand different strains of bacteria in and on the body. Only consuming a few strains of probiotics would be like choosing two vegetables to eat for the rest of your life. When you limit the variety in your life, you limit the benefits. Different strains of bacteria are responsible for different functions. So, by deductive reasoning, getting a greater variety is always best.

On top of that, kefir averages 6-10 different strains of healthy yeasts.[80] Healthy yeasts aren't talked about very often, but the yeasts found in kefir promote health in their own unique ways. For example, they have specifically been shown to improve the condition of infections as well as increase your body's ability to retain short chain fatty acids*. Another significant function of the yeasts is that, because they have a symbiotic relationship with the bacteria, the yeast improves the viability of the bacteria to survive the gastric juices in the stomach*. Other cultured dairy foods don't usually contain any of these yeasts, thus again making kefir superior in many ways.

Lastly, let's chat about survivability. Probiotics, in order to be effective, have to survive the journey through the stomach acid in order to reach the large intestine. This is where 90% of bacteria "hang out" and do their job. So, for any probiotic to make it there, it has to NOT get killed by the harsh environment in the stomach. One researcher isolated 58 bacteria strains in kefir and incubated them for four hours in a vat of bile salt (pH 2.5).[81] They did this to mimic the stomach environment, as these probiotics would have to do in the digestive process. The cool part: ALL 58 strains of bacteria survived. Of those, 85% of the strains showed resistance to the harsh environment, but had delayed growth, meaning they didn't grow in numbers when they were in the bile salt, but they survived—which is all you need to deliver those bugs to your gut. How cool is that! Kefir, because it's made in milk, has the ability to coat the stomach and protect the bacteria as it passes through. This is what makes kefir unique to many other fermented foods. It provides the perfect vehicle for delivering the greatest amount of probiotics healthy and alive.

Signed, sealed, delivered—and totally untainted by the hand of man.

Chapter Twenty

So, What?

A Brief Summary

Like any teacher worth her salt, I'm going to briefly review what we've talked about with the hope that, if you don't already, you'll start to see how all of this comes together.

Your gut is the most overlooked part of your body when it comes to the choices you make and the health you feel as a result. For whatever reason, perhaps because our guts are so good at running on autopilot, we just don't give them the time and thought we should. We have social stigmas about poop, farts, bowel movements, and bellies in general. But, ask anyone whose health has taken a turn for the worse due to a lack of gut health, and you'll soon learn that your gut has everything to do with how you feel.

Our guts are incredibly complex and are connected to nearly every other bodily system. More than just poop, gas, and food, our guts contribute—in a major way—to our mood, cravings, immune system, body weight, thinking ability, and more. Our guts are home to billions and trillions of tiny little organisms—bacteria—that work to keep us healthy. In opposition to most people's assumptions, much of the bacteria in the world is good for us! The more good bacteria we have, the less susceptible we are to bad bacteria. Good gut microbiota are absolutely essential for a healthy, vibrant, and disease free life. There's no getting around it—we need those bugs!

In a world full of artificial materials created over the centuries, kefir stands unique as a 100% natural "food" that seems to have no other purpose in its existence than to produce a substance that blesses the life of mankind by infusing our bodies with vibrant, wholly natural probiotics. Paradoxically, kefir has bewildered scientists, while at the same time having its many benefits confirmed by them. It's fun and easy to make, can be used in nearly endless ways, and you never need rely on any company, lab, or store to keep you in supply of it. Once you have your grains and a glass of milk, there truly are no barriers to entry. Kefir's benefits are available to every man, woman, and child brave enough to drink this warm milk.

What Else Can You Do with Five Minutes?

Recently I saw a TV commercial that fades into this really beautiful outdoor shot with a middle-aged man doing a single pushup in super slow motion. He does this pushup with absolutely perfect form, chiseled muscles showing clearly on the screen—you know the kind. The narrator says something like, "If you could get heart health with just one pushup, would you do it?" The commercial is evidently an advertisement for a pharmaceutical company and is supposed to make you think that their product is the easiest thing you can do to get some heart health benefits. Obviously your heart won't really be healthier with just one pushup, but they want you to think that taking their pill will fix your heart problems (and give you chiseled muscles).

While I may not agree with the message behind the "power of just one pill," I have to admit, when I saw this ad it did make me think of kefir. Why? Because drinking a single glass of kefir will make you ripped out of your mind.

No it won't.

But, it can help!

Seriously though, the question of, "What else can you do with five minutes that will drastically change your life?" seems to be tailor-made for kefir. What else can you do in five minutes a day to improve your health? Certainly not pushups. I should probably do a few more pushups every day, but that wouldn't have cured my lactose intolerance. I could run for five minutes a day, but that wouldn't keep my acid reflux at bay. You could even spend five minutes chewing on some leafy greens. And while those are super nutritious, it doesn't pack the punch of probiotics for your gut health like kefir does.

Kefir isn't the kind of thing that takes months and years to show results. As previously mentioned, a single cup of kefir contains more probiotic punch than literally anything else you could consume. Instead of a "single pushup" or a "single pill," what if you simply drank a single cup of kefir each morning? I would argue, and the research backs me up, that no other seemingly small, five-minute task could possesses the same health- and life-changing potential as that cup of kefir—especially if you're suffering from particularly severe gut-related illness. Are you going to feel like Superman or Wonder Woman fifteen minutes after it goes down your gullet? Probably not. But, you may be surprised just how quickly you start to notice a change.

The Best Thing You've Never Heard Of

We just spent 50,000 words with each other—that practically makes us family, right? I'd like to pose a question that, perhaps, is a bit odd: If you were to close the cover of this book—right now—and a friend of yours were to then walk up and ask what this book is about, what would you tell them?

Before you read any further, I'd like you to stop and think about that for a second.

Based on what you've read, what would you say this book is about?

Would you say it's a book about kefir? Would you say it's a book about digestion? The gut? Bacteria? Disease? Being healthy?

To me, this question reveals one of the coolest parts about books, and writing in general: Often, the message I had in mind as the writer and the message you internalize as the reader are two different things—and I love that. What it means is that the words I wrote and the words you read, though technically the same, are interpreted differently based upon the circumstances in life in which you find yourself. My life, my health, and my experiences are different than yours. I can't, and never will, pretend to perfectly understand who you are and what you're going through. But, as I mentioned at the beginning of the book, my intent in writing this labor of love is this: to help you—whomever you are—feel better.

I would venture to guess that you found your way to these words because you've experienced pain, disease, dysbiosis, or something of the like. If you're human, you've experienced at least one of those things sometime throughout your life. And my ultimate goal—my reason for writing—is to help you, at least in some way, experience less pain and less disease because of your newfound knowledge of the healing power found in kefir, probiotics, and a healthy gut microbiota.

I want to reemphasize it one more time: <u>These kefir grains have the capacity to make your life better.</u> And, if you can overcome some of the preconceived notions you may have about bacteria, warm milk, and fermentation, I know kefir can offer a life-changing difference to your health, a difference you probably didn't even know was possible.

I've heard kefir described as, "The best thing you've never heard of—Nature's hidden miracle."

I love that description because, for me, it couldn't be more true. I know it will be the same for you.

Let's Keep in Touch

Do you have any questions? Is your head spinning? Do you have specific health concerns you're wondering about? If so, please don't let our conversation end here. Seriously, if you need anything, if you're confused, or need answers to any kefir question, please reach out to me. Visit me on my website: www.KefirLove.com. Send me an email, leave me a comment, or follow me on Instagram @kefirlove. It's my goal to reply to everyone who sends me a message. I'd love to hear from you!

Part Three

Recipes and Resources

Chapter Twenty-One

Quick Reference Guide

FAQ: Kefir & Kefir Grains

Q: What is kefir?

A: Kefir is a cultured dairy drink. It is made most commonly from cow's milk but can be made from goat or sheep milk. For dairy-free options, there are two choices: there is a water kefir variety made with sugar water, or it can be made with milk alternatives, (soy milk, coconut milk etc). All kefir is made with a starter called a kefir "grain". These grains are not actually a grain—like wheat or rice. Rather, it is a sugar and protein structure that houses a colony of healthy bacteria and yeasts. When these grains are placed in milk, they infuse the milk with probiotics that promote gut healing and health.

Q: What strains of bacteria does kefir contain?

A: Kefir contains mostly lactobacillus, bifidobacterium and acetobacter.

Q: What's the difference between milk kefir and water kefir?

A: Milk kefir uses milk kefir grains. This type of kefir is made from grains that consume lactose in milk. Water kefir uses a different SCOBY, called water kefir grains, and they consume the sugar found in the water base. They have similar bacteria strains, but are slightly different, and milk kefir has about 3X the probiotic diversity and potency of water kefir.

Q: Is a kefir grain a SCOBY?

A: Yes, a kefir grain is a Symbiotic Culture of Bacteria and Yeast. It infuses both healthy bacteria and yeasts into the milk.

Q: Does milk kefir have gluten?

A: No. Kefir is gluten-free.

Q: What nutrients are in kefir?

A: Kefir is full of vitamins A, D, B12 and B6. It has more calcium than milk, and a healthy dose of phosphorus, magnesium, and potassium.

Q: Are milk kefir grains reusable?

A: Yes. Milk kefir grains are strained from each batch and placed into the next batch for culturing. They can last indefinitely if well taken care of.

Q: What is a powdered kefir starter culture?

A: There are some powdered starters available to purchase. These powders are made for convenience, but lack the power contained in a real kefir grain. They are often made from dehydrated, ground kefir grains but may include other products inside each individual packet. When you make kefir with this starter, the powder is poured into a fresh glass of milk. The powder then ferments the milk over a 24-hour period. It is usually a 1-time use product.

Q: My kefir grains float to the top of the jar. Is that normal?

A: Yes, this is normal. Because kefir grains produce CO2, it gives them the buoyancy to float to the top of the milk in the jar. This means they are healthy and actively fermenting your milk.

FAQ: Making Kefir

Q: How long should it take to make kefir?

A: It should take around 24 hours to fully ferment a batch of kefir. It is normal for kefir to ferment between 12 to 48 hours.

Q: Will kefir make my jar explode if I tighten a lid?

A: Technically, kefir does produce CO2, but it is likely not strong enough to break the jar. I always tighten my lids and have never had a problem with explosion. Burping, or periodically loosening the jar to release pressure, can help prevent any issues.

Q: What do I do if my house is colder than 68 degrees?

A: If your house is consistently 68 degrees or cooler, then you may not get optimal results for each kefir batch. Kefir does best if fermented between 72-78 degrees. If turning up the heat is not an option, then look for warms spots in your house, not in direct sunlight. This may be on top of a fridge, the oven light (be sure not to turn the oven on!), a cupboard, or by a candle warmer or other running device.

Q: Do I need to stir the kefir as it ferments?

A: No. Stirring it will speed up the process significantly. It is best to allow the grains to do their work in their own time.

Q: How do I know if I've successfully made kefir?

A: Look for clues that the milk has turned into kefir. Kefir will have a thick consistency, start producing little bubbles or pockets of whey, usually at the bottom of the jar.

Q: How do I know if it's gone bad or is full of bad bacteria?

A: Kefir and other cultured foods are safe to consume once the pH gets to between 4.0 and 4.5. The best thing to do is follow your nose. If your kefir smells really off suddenly, or contains mold in strange colors, then its best to throw that batch out.

Q: What should my kefir taste like?

A: Kefir has a creamy texture, a tart taste, and a slightly yeasty aroma.

Q: Should I rinse my grains with water between batches?

A: No! Kefir grains retain a milky/jelly-like layer on the outside. This is completely full of bacteria, ready to kick start the next batch of kefir. Rinsing grains is detrimental to their productivity.

Q: Can I use UHT/UP milk?

A: No. Ultra-heat-treatment and ultra pasteurized milk are not good for making kefir or for the kefir grains.

Q: Are there dairy free options?

A: Yes! Milk kefir grains can be placed into coconut milk or milk alternatives for 1-3 batches of fermentation. After that, they must be returned to real milk for 2-3 batches to maintain their health.

Q: Can I use non-homogenized milk for my kefir?

A: Yes. If you use non-homogonized milk for your kefir, the cream will collect on the top where the kefir grains usually hang out. Just be sure to fish the grains out and give your milk a stir before you drink.

Q: Can I use raw milk to make kefir?

A: Yes. Using raw milk is quite popular. This is because raw milk has lots of digestive enzymes and healthy bacteria already, which when paired with kefir, makes quite the healthy drink.

Q: How do I take a break from making kefir?

A: If you need to take a break from kefir, then simply put your grains in a jar of milk and place them in the fridge. This should last 2-3 weeks before the milk needs to be replaced. Having them in the fridge longer than 2-3 months will harm the grains.

Q: Can I make kefir once or twice a week and then keep them in the refrigerator the rest of the days?

A: it is not recommended that you use this method. Kefir grains thrive best with consistency, so constantly changing their temperature can be detrimental and leave your grains weak. It is better to find a ratio that works well for you and your schedule, or look into powdered starters for kefir if you are going to be making kefir very inconsistently. For me, I try and make 2 cups of kefir every day. That is enough to supply my family and I on a daily basis.

FAQ: After Your Batch is Done

Q: How often should I clean the jar I use for making kefir?

A: The jar you use to ferment kefir in should be washed 1-2 times a week. It does not have to be washed every day, in fact, the residue in the jar is full of bacteria that will help jump start the next batch.

Q: What do I do with extra kefir grains?

A: Extra kefir grains have many uses. First, they are completely safe to consume! While it may not sound appetizing to snack on them or put them on a salad, throwing them in a smoothie is a great way to get an extra probiotic boost. If I'm not sharing extra grains with friends, I like to feed them to my dog. They are also great to throw into compost piles, too.

Q: How do I make kefir cheese?

A: Kefir cheese must be made by straining the whey out of the kefir. This is done using something like cheese cloth, coffee filters or nut-milk bags. See the attendant chapter dedicated to this topic.

Q: What can I do with the whey after I make cheese?

A: Whey is the translucent golden liquid that separates from the milk when you make cheese. It is full of nutrients, proteins, and enzymes. It can be used as the liquid base of a smoothie, an alternative to any water requirement for a recipe, or can be used as the perfect medium for fermenting your own fruits and veggies.

Q: How much kefir can I drink a day?

A: As much as you want! There really isn't a "too much" limit when it comes to probiotics. Your gut will thrive off the newcomers when you start drinking kefir. Just remember that kefir is an ultra dense food, even when it comes to calories. So make sure it fits in your overall nutrition plan. Personally, I drink 1 cup of kefir every day.

Q: Is kefir safe for children to drink?

A: Yes. I began feeding kefir to my daughter when she was about 8 months old. Be sure to start with very small amounts—even a teaspoon a day at the beginning test it out. Because kefir has a slight alcohol content, you want to make sure to use mild ferments on young children. But make sure you talk to your child's pediatrician too about any concerns you may have.

Troubleshooting Tips

Q: My grains don't appear to be working. What do I do?

A: If, after 24 hours, your grains don't appear to be working, strain the milk and assess your grains. If they are "dead" they will appear to be a slightly darker color and look more like crystals than cauliflower florets. "Dead" grains will lose that gelatinous membrane (slimy coating) on the outside and will look hard, not squishy. To bring kefir grains back to life, put them in 1-2 cups of milk and be sure to place them in a warm spot out of direct sunlight (74-76 degrees if possible). The warm will encourage the bacteria to grow again. Do this every 24 hours until the grains revive. Remember, kefir grains are very resilient. I've had grains that look completely dead and dried come back to full power within just a few days. Consistency is key.

Q: My kefir has separated into curds and whey? Why did this happen?

A: A separation of curds and whey mean that the kefir has over-fermented. This does not mean the kefir is ruined, it's just not optimal for your tasting pleasure. The acidity of the fermentation caused the milk to curdle, just like lemon juice makes milk curdle.

Q: I've made kefir for a while now, but the taste has changed. What do I do?

A: Kefir grains sometimes have a mind of their own. As easy as a culture they are to keep alive, they are certainly difficult to peg down sometimes. Even a slight change in temperature, one that is barely imperceptible to you, can alter the way kefir grains ferment the milk. Kefir grains can even be sensitive to changes in milk brands. First check to make sure the grains are active, and there is no visible mold inside your fermentation jar. Continue with the routine or try changing grains.

Q: My kefir is too runny. What can I do to make it thicker?

A: Remember that kefiran is the thickening agent in kefir. This is produced from a bacteria inside the grain. Because of this, you just have to make sure that the bacteria in your grains are healthy and thriving. If the milk hasn't fermented long enough, it won't be thick. If the milk has fermented to long, it can be runny. Straining the grains from the kefir before the whey starts to separate is important in getting just the right thickness.

Q: My kefir smells like yeast. Is this normal?

A: All milk kefir has a yeast in it, so it's normal for it to smell yeasty. If the yeast smell is overpowering or particularly stronger than it used to be, this is not optimal. Kefir should have a balance of tartness and yeastiness. This means that there is a balance of bacteria and yeast inside the kefir. If your kefir grains smell extremely yeasty, then the yeast may be dominating the culture, becoming stronger than the bacteria. As long as your milk is showing signs of fermentation and thickening, then it is safe to consume.

Q: What do I do with curds and whey?

A: It is still safe to consume curds and whey. Remember Little Miss Muffet? Simply strain the grains and give it a good quick whisk. The kefir won't be smooth in texture had it not separated, so that's why I like to throw this kefir into smoothies so I will never notice. Or you can throw away the curds and save the whey. It will not have quite as an acidic taste as the curds.

Q: My kefir is fermenting too quickly. What do I do?

A: Kefir ferments quickly when it is very warm and if the jar is agitated/stirred often, OR if there are too many grains inside. Kefir will ferment much quicker in warm summer months. In changes of season you will find that you have to adjust the ratio of grains quite frequently as the temperature changes adjust.

Q: My kefir is fermenting too slow. How can I speed it up?

A: Slow kefir can be due to cold temperatures or unhealthy grains. Try finding slightly warmer place for it to sit and ferment, OR give it 1-2 quick stirs in the middle of the ferment. This will help infuse the bacteria and yeasts more quickly.

Q: I left my kefir fermenting on the counter for several days. Are my grains still okay?

A: Your grains will likely survive, yes. Get them into fresh milk as soon as possible and allow a few days to get them back up to speed.

Q: I accidentally dropped my grains on the floor. What should I do?

A: A simple check will do. If there are any particles on them, try rinsing with milk first in your strainer. If this gets all the debris off, then great. Rinsing thoroughly with water should be a last resort option for trying to save your grains.

Q: I see pink or brown patches on my kefir grains and in the jar. What is this?

A: If you see any abnormal color on your kefir grains or in your kefir jar, it is likely mold. Do not consume this kefir. If it is on your kefir grains, gently rinse the kefir grains until they are free of mold and return to milk. Dump the next 2-3 batches until you are confident your kefir has returned to normal.

Chapter Twenty-Two

Smoothie Recipes

These are super simple! Combine all ingredients into a blender and blend until smooth. Drink immediately for best probiotic results.

Strawberry Coconut Kefir

2 cups coconut milk kefir
1/4 cup pureed strawberries

> Put your grains in coconut milk for 24 hours to ferment. (Your grains may take more than one batch to adjust. If you normally make kefir with cow, goat or sheep milk, give it a few days to adjust to the new coconut milk). Mix chilled coconut kefir with 1/4 cup pureed strawberries until combined. Enjoy!

Orange Julius Kefir Smoothie

2 cups kefir
1 cup fresh squeezed orange juice
1/2 tsp vanilla
1 Tb pure maple syrup
1/2 cup ice

Cran-Apple Kefir Smoothie

1 cup kefir
1/2 unsweetened applesauce
1/2 cup whole, fresh cranberries
1 cup spinach
1/2 cup ice
Dash of cinnamon

Mango Kefir Smoothie

1 cup kefir
1 cup freshly squeezed orange juice
1/3 cup frozen blueberries
1/2 cup frozen mango
1/4 cup coconut
1 cup spinach
3-5 slices of cucumber
1 Tb coconut nectar syrup

Green Goddess Kefir Smoothie

2 cups kefir
2 cups leafy greens (spinach, kale, swiss chard, etc)
1/2 cucumber
1/2 frozen banana
1 pear
1/3 cup raw pecans

Nutty Kefir Smoothie

2 cups kefir
1 frozen banana
2 Tb almond butter
2 Tb flax seed
1 tsp vanilla extract
1 cup ice

Morning Moo Kefir Smoothie

2 cups kefir
1/2 frozen banana
1/2 cup oats
1 Tb. Raw cocoa powder
1 Tb honey
1 Tb chia seeds
Handful of ice

Post-Workout Kefir Smoothie

2 cups kefir
1 frozen banana
2 scoops chocolate protein powder (any variety will do)
2 Tb peanut butter
Handful of ice

Chocolate Milk Kefir

2 cups kefir
2-4 Tb. organic chocolate syrup

Stir or Mix, then serve cold!

Coconut Banana Kefir Smoothie

2 cups coconut milk kefir
1 frozen banana
4 Tb raw hemp seeds
4 Tb dried coconut
Handful of ice

Chapter Twenty-Three

Second Ferments

A second ferment is a fantastic way to give your kefir an extra probiotic kick!

It's really simple: All you do is make your regular kefir. But, after you have removed the kefir grains, you take your fresh kefir and leave it in a glass jar on your countertop for another 4-24 hours. This is called the second ferment. What it does is allows the existing probiotics in the kefir to continue to grow, even without the grains.

Remember that this happens right after the grains are removed. Don't do this with kefir that has already been sitting in the fridge for a few days. A second ferment is best done when the bacteria is thriving at its peak levels. I find even just a few hours will give my kefir enough time to continue to culture. Leaving a second ferment out too long can over-ferment your kefir, so keep an eye on it before the whey starts to separate.

This is a perfect time to infuse all sorts of flavors into your kefir, without actually blending it in. For example, you can place an orange peel, slices of fruit or whole herbs into your kefir. When the second ferment is done, you remove the flavoring agent, but the kefir will still take on those flavors for an excellent drink.

Recap: How to Make the Second Ferment

1. Make your kefir, following your normal routine.
2. Remove the kefir grains.
3. Replace the fresh kefir into a jar (no kefir grains!).
4. If flavoring, place ingredients into the jar along with the kefir.
5. Tighten the lid! This gives your kefir a lovely fizz.
6. Leave on countertop for another 4-24 hours
7. Remove or strain the ingredients added during the second ferment

Be sure to give it a quick whisk before you drink to blend the flavors. :)

Below are second ferment recipes that are just delicious. It's one of my favorite ways to flavor kefir and experiment with all sorts of infused flavors!

Second Ferment Recipes

Berry Kefir

Place a handful of blackberries in 2-4 cups of freshly strained kefir. Leave the jar of berries and kefir on your countertop for 4-12 hours. Strain the berries OR blend them up like a smoothie.

Orange Kefir

Peel a fresh orange. Put half the peel in 2-4 cups of freshly strained kefir. Leave the jar of kefir and orange peel on your countertop for 4-12 hours. Remove the orange peel before drinking!

Cinnamon & Clove Kefir

Place 1/2 cinnamon stick and 1-2 cloves in freshly strained kefir. 2nd ferment for 4-12 hours. Strain the cinnamon stick and cloves from the kefir, do not eat these ingredients!

Chai Tea Kefir

Steep a chai tea bag (or any of your favs) into 2-4 cups of kefir and 2nd ferment for 4-12 hours. Remove the tea bag, making sure no remnants of the bag or spices are left in the kefir.

Lemon Basil Kefir

Place 2-3 slices of lemon and 1-3 basil leaves into your freshly strained kefir. Second ferment for 4-12 hours. Strain the lemon and basil out of the kefir. Enjoy!

Blackberry Lemon Kefir

Place a handful of fresh blackberries (sliced in half) and 2 slices of lemon into your freshly strained kefir. Second ferment for 4-12 hours. Strain the blackberries and lemons and serve!

Chapter Twenty-Four

Water Kefir Recipes

For more information on Water Kefir, see chapter 16.

Traditional Water Kefir

Mix 1/4 cup of organic sugar into 1 quart boiling water until completely dissolved. Let the sugar water cool completely. Once it is cooled, add kefir grains, a whole lemon cut into quarter pieces, and 1 dried fig. Ferment for 24 hours before removing the lemon and fig. Strain the kefir grains and set aside for new batch. Drink the fresh water kefir right away, or store in the refrigerator.

Ginger Water Kefir

Add 1/4 cup organic sugar into 1 quart boiling water until completely dissolved. Let the sugar water cool completely. Once it is cooled, add kefir grains, 1 cube of fresh, peeled ginger. Add 1/2 lemon cut into pieces. Ferment for 24 hours and strain everything out.

Water Kefir Lemonade

Make water kefir, and remove the grains. Add 1/4 cup of lemon juice to 1 quart of water kefir. Sweeten if desired and serve cold!

Pomegranate Water Kefir

Make water kefir, and remove the grains. Pour 1/4 cup of pomegranate juice unto water kefir. Seal tightly and ferment on your countertop for another 24 hours (or until you get the desired kefir).

Apple-Beer Kefir Soda

Make water kefir and remove the grains. Mix equal parts of water kefir and apple juice. Pour into an airtight container and leave on countertop for another 24 hours for a bubbly apple-beer soda!

Herbal Water Kefir

Make water kefir, and remove the grains. Add herbal infused water to water kefir in equal parts. Boil herbs in water and let them steep for several hours. Pour desired amount of herbal infused water into your water kefir.

Coconut Raspberry Kefir Ice-Pops

Make coconut water kefir, and remove the grains. Put coconut water kefir & fresh raspberries into blender or food processor until you get desired consistency. Pour into popsicle molds and freeze!

Chapter Twenty-Five

How to Make Kefir Cheese

Cheese is typically made by culturing milk by adding bacteria or enzymes and then strained to a dense consistency. The clear liquid that is strained off is called whey. The more whey that can be separated from the cheese, the harder the cheese will be. Straining the whey off is done by using some type of cheese cloth, nut milk bag or coffee filter.

To do this with kefir, you first line a strainer/colander with the cheese cloth. Put a bowl underneath the strainer/colander to catch the whey that will drip from the kefir. Pour the kefir into the cheese cloth-lined bowl. What's left in your strainer will be cheese. Underneath, in the bowl catching the drippings is whey. Don't throw this golden, translucent stuff away, though! It is full of nutrients, probiotics too! It's called sweet whey, and it can be used in bread baking, put in smoothies to be consumed, or used to ferment veggies!

The really important part about making kefir cheese is that it will continue to ferment even after you start straining the kefir. The first few times I did this my kefir cheese smelled more like nail polish than anything resembling a dairy product. To keep it from fermenting further while you wait for it to strain, simply put it in the fridge! By letting your cheese strain in the fridge, you slow the fermentation down and the whey will continue to seep out. The end result is a tart, but creamy cheese that can add a bit of acidity and creaminess to any dish.

Always put the kefir in the fridge while it is straining. By keeping it in the fridge, it allows the fermenting to slow down enough that you won't get over-fermented cheese. If you leave the kefir out while it strains, it just ferments at the same rate it was doing so before, so the result is a VERY bitter and acidic cheese. Also, plan on a 50-75% reduction in mass. 1 quart of kefir will not give you 1 quart of kefir cheese.

Soft Kefir Cheese

1 quart of freshly strained kefir
1-2 Tb fresh herbs (like chives) if you wish

Stir the herbs into the kefir. Pour this mixture over your straining cloth. Cover and put it into the fridge for 12-24 hours. Squeeze any extra whey you can until you get the consistency you wish. This should resemble a cheese similar to a soft cream cheese, but will have a more tart taste.

Hard Kefir Cheese

1 quart of freshly strained kefir

To make a hard kefir cheese, follow the same previous steps. The goal is to simply get more whey out of the kefir. To do this, wrap the soft kefir cheese into a cheese cloth. Place a plate on top of the cheese cloth and weigh down the plate with something heavy like a canned food item. Be creative ;) Put more weight on the plate every few hours until no whey comes dripping out of the cheese. This should leave you with a hard cheese that may be a little crumbly when grated. Serve it over salads or grate it over pasta.

Kefir Sour Cream

1 carton of heavy cream

Simply replace the milk you would use for making a batch of kefir with heavy cream. Place your kefir grains into the heavy cream. Allow the heavy cream to ferment until it is thicker and creamy. This may take longer than milk because of the increased fat content. If your strainer isn't effective in removing the grains, then wash your hands and just use your fingers! Use this in place of sour cream on any dish you desire.

Chapter Twenty-Six

Kefir Skin Care

Putting kefir on your face may seem weird, and I won't lie—it is. It's SO weird to put food on your face and call it a good idea. However, I wouldn't tell you to try this if it didn't feel amazing, I promise. It's an all-natural face mask with really simple ingredients that you probably already have. This recipe will keep your skin hydrated, refreshed, balanced, and SO clear.

Kefir: Kefir contains 30+ strains of good bacteria to supplement your natural skin biome. It contains alpha hydroxy acid (AHA) which restores pH of the skin, and also reduces fine lines and wrinkles.

Coconut Oil: Great natural base for beauty products, is extremely hydrating.

Lemon Juice: Lemon juice is an antibacterial so is great for treating breakouts. It removes excess oils and also contains vitamin C and citric acid which restores skin pigmentation and enhances your complexion.

Honey: Honey contains essential nutrients, is very hydrating, and creates a natural glow. For best results, use raw and unpasteurized, local honey.

Just a few tips: all ingredients should be at room temperature before mixing. It is difficult to mix if chilled or cooled. Likewise, if the ingredients are warmed, or are too hot, it will become too runny to create a face mask. I always use strained kefir to get it really thick. If you put 1/4 cup of freshly strained kefir over a coffee filter 6-12 hours before, it will get that thick consistency that makes it such a creamy mask.

Kefir Face Mask

1 TB thick Kefir
1 TB softened coconut oil
1 tsp honey
1/2 tsp lemon juice

    Mix all ingredients at room temperature. Spread mixture over your face and let sit 10 minutes to 1 hour. If you have extra, apply a second coat after the first coat dries. Rinse, wash, and hydrate for a beautifully healthy (and natural) glow.

Would You Mind Helping Me with Something?

I want to thank you for buying my book. I appreciate it more than you know.

As you can probably tell, I wholeheartedly believe in the healing power of kefir and its ability to change lives. I can tell you, with full confidence, that if you incorporate it into your life, you'll begin to start feeling better in a genuine and substantial way.

Would you mind helping me with something? As you might imagine, writers such as myself pour their souls into their work. I've dedicated thousands of hours of my life to this book and, if you've found something useful, helpful, or enlightening, would you please let me know?

If you've got an extra 5 minutes, would you write a little review for me on Amazon.com? I read all of my reviews, and I'd love to know if my book helped you in any way. Truthfully, that's the payoff for all of this research—knowing I had a hand in helping someone else.

Also, if you happened to think of someone else while reading, and thought they may enjoy kefir, probiotics, and the wellness they offer, will you pass this book along to them? It would mean a lot!

Much love,

- Whit

About the Author

Having earned a Bachelor's Degree in Early Childhood and Special Education from Brigham Young University Idaho, and a M.Ed. from Utah State University, Whitney Wilson quickly developed a passion for helping others through research. A lifelong learner, Whitney grew up in Idaho and Oregon, eventually moving to Salt Lake City, Utah to complete her education where she worked in the public-school system for many years.

An avid reader, researcher, and writer, Whitney currently operates the website www.KefirLove.com where she shares her passion for cultured food, probiotics, and natural wellness on a daily basis.

Whitney and her family, including their mangy, bearded dog Rue currently make their home in Salt Lake City, Utah USA.

Medical Disclaimer

I'm not a doctor, nor do I play one on T.V.

The information found in this book is not meant to, or implied to be, a substitute for professional medical advice, diagnosis or treatment. All content, including text, graphics, images and information, contained in, or available through, this book is for general information purposes only.

I strongly encourage you to confirm any information obtained from this book with other sources, and review all information regarding any medical condition or treatment with your physician.

NEVER DISREGARD PROFESSIONAL MEDICAL ADVICE OR DELAY SEEKING MEDICAL TREATMENT BECAUSE OF SOMETHING YOU HAVE READ ON OR ACCESSED THROUGH THIS BOOK.

References

1 https://www.cdc.gov/chronicdisease/overview/index.htm

2 Dominguez-Bello, M. G., Costello, E. K., Contreras, M., Magris, M., Hidalgo, G., Fierer, N., & Knight, R. (2010). Delivery mode shapes the acquisition and structure of the initial microbiota across multiple body habitats in newborns. Proceedings of the National Academy of Sciences, 107(26), 11971-11975.

3 Harmsen, H. J., Wildeboer–Veloo, A. C., Raangs, G. C., Wagendorp, A. A., Klijn, N., Bindels, J. G., & Welling, G. W. (2000). Analysis of intestinal flora development in breast-fed and formula-fed infants by using molecular identification and detection methods. Journal of pediatric gastroenterology and nutrition, 30(1), 61-67.

4 Fujimura, K. E., Johnson, C. C., Ownby, D. R., Cox, M. J., Brodie, E. L., Havstad, S. L., ... & Boushey, H. A. (2010). Man's best friend? The effect of pet ownership on house dust microbial communities. The Journal of allergy and clinical immunology, 126(2), 410.

D. R., Johnson, C. C., & Peterson, E. L. (2002). Exposure to dogs and cats in the first year of life and risk of allergic sensitization at 6 to 7 years of age. Jama, 288(8), 963-972.

A. M., Davis, M. F., Tyldsley, A. S., Hodkinson, B. P., Tolomeo, P., Hu, B., ... & Grice, E. A. (2015). The shared microbiota of humans and companion animals as evaluated from Staphylococcus carriage sites. Microbiome, 3(1), 2.

5 Yatsunenko, T., Rey, F. E., Manary, M. J., Trehan, I., Dominguez-Bello, M. G., Contreras, M., ... & Heath, A. C. (2012). Human gut microbiome viewed across age and geography. nature, 486(7402), 222.

6 Quigley, E. M. (2013). Gut bacteria in health and disease. Gastroenterology & hepatology, 9(9), 560.

7 http://americannutritionassociation.org/newsletter/science-probiotics

8. http://www.parentingscience.com/prebiotics.html#sthash.zpzjhF5H.dpuf

9 Holscher HD, Faust KL, Czerkies LA, Litov R, Ziegler EE, Lessin H, Hatch T, Sun S, and Tappenden KA. 2012. Effects of prebiotic-containing infant formula on gastrointestinal tolerance and fecal microbiota in a randomized controlled trial. JPEN J Parenter Enteral Nutr. 36(1 Suppl):95S-105S.

10 https://www.niddk.nih.gov/health-information/health-statistics/digestive-diseases

11 Vrieze, A., Van Nood, E., Holleman, F., Salojärvi, J., Kootte, R. S., Bartelsman, J. F., ... & Derrien, M. (2012). Transfer of intestinal microbiota from lean donors increases insulin sensitivity in individuals with metabolic syndrome. Gastroenterology, 143(4), 913-916.

12 Salonen, A., de Vos, W. M., & Palva, A. (2010). Gastrointestinal microbiota in irritable bowel syndrome: present state and perspectives. Microbiology, 156(11), 3205-

3215.

13 Saulnier, D. M., Riehle, K., Mistretta, T. A., Diaz, M. A., Mandal, D., Raza, S., ... & Petrosino, J. F. (2011). Gastrointestinal microbiome signatures of pediatric patients with irritable bowel syndrome. Gastroenterology, 141(5), 1782-1791.

14 Mearin, F., Cucala, M., Azpiroz, F., & Malagelada, J. R. (1991). The origin of symptoms on the brain-gut axis in functional dyspepsia. Gastroenterology, 101(4), 999-1006.

15 Mearin, F., Cucala, M., Azpiroz, F., & Malagelada, J. R. (1991). The origin of symptoms on the brain-gut axis in functional dyspepsia. Gastroenterology, 101(4), 999-1006.

16 Faria, A., & Weiner, H. L. (2005). Oral tolerance. Immunological reviews, 206(1), 232-259.

17 Vighi, G., Marcucci, F., Sensi, L., Di Cara, G., & Frati, F. (2008). Allergy and the gastrointestinal system. Clinical & Experimental Immunology, 153(s1), 3-6

18 Dunlop, B. W., & Nemeroff, C. B. (2007). The role of dopamine in the pathophysiology of depression. Archives of general psychiatry, 64(3), 327-337.

19 Bajbouj, M., Merkl, A., Schlaepfer, T. E., Frick, C., Zobel, A., Maier, W., ... & Rau, H. (2010). Two-year outcome of vagus nerve stimulation in treatment-resistant depression. Journal of clinical psychopharmacology, 30(3), 273-281.

20 Mulle, J. G., Sharp, W. G., & Cubells, J. F. (2013). The gut microbiome: a new frontier in autism research. Current psychiatry reports, 15(2), 337.

Krajmalnik-Brown, R., Lozupone, C., Kang, D. W., & Adams, J. B. (2015). Gut bacteria in children with autism spectrum disorders: challenges and promise of studying how a complex community influences a complex disease. Microbial ecology in health and disease, 26(1), 26914.

21 Sampson, T. R., & Mazmanian, S. K. (2015). Control of brain development, function, and behavior by the microbiome. Cell host & microbe, 17(5), 565-576.

22 Spor, A., Koren, O., & Ley, R. (2011). Unravelling the effects of the environment and host genotype on the gut microbiome. Nature reviews. Microbiology, 9(4), 279.

23 Sclafani, A., Ackroff, K., & Abumrad, N. A. (2007). CD36 gene deletion reduces fat preference and intake but not post-oral fat conditioning in mice. American Journal of Physiology-Regulatory, Integrative and Comparative Physiology, 293(5), R1823-R1832.

24 Stefka, A. T., Feehley, T., Tripathi, P., Qiu, J., McCoy, K., Mazmanian, S. K., ... & Antonopoulos, D. A. (2014). Commensal bacteria protect against food allergen sensitization. Proceedings of the National Academy of Sciences, 111(36), 13145-13150.

25 Abrams, S. A., Griffin, I. J., Hawthorne, K. M., & Ellis, K. J. (2007). Effect of prebiotic supplementation and calcium intake on body mass index. The Journal of pediatrics, 151(3), 293-298.

26 Cani, P. D., Lecourt, E., Dewulf, E. M., Sohet, F. M., Pachikian, B. D., Naslain, D., ... & Delzenne, N. M. (2009). Gut microbiota fermentation of prebiotics increases satietogenic

and incretin gut peptide production with consequences for appetite sensation and glucose response after a meal. The American journal of clinical nutrition, 90(5), 1236-1243.

27 https://www.cdc.gov/mmwr/preview/mmwrhtml/mm4829a1.htm

28 https://www.fda.gov/downloads/ForIndustry/UserFees/AnimalDrugUserFeeActADUFA/UCM231851.pdf

29 Rickman, J. C., Barrett, D. M., & Bruhn, C. M. (2007). Nutritional comparison of fresh, frozen and canned fruits and vegetables. Part 1. Vitamins C and B and phenolic compounds. Journal of the Science of Food and Agriculture, 87(6), 930-944.

30 https://www.cdc.gov/drugresistance/threat-report-2013/index.html

31 Scott, F. I., Horton, D. B., Mamtani, R., Haynes, K., Goldberg, D. S., Lee, D. Y., & Lewis, J. D. (2016). Administration of antibiotics to children before age 2 years increases risk for childhood obesity. Gastroenterology, 151(1), 120-129.

Jernberg, C., Löfmark, S., Edlund, C., & Jansson, J. K. (2010). Long-term impacts of antibiotic exposure on the human intestinal microbiota. Microbiology, 156(11), 3216-3223.

32 Lopitz-Otsoa, F., Rementeria, A., Elguezabal, N., & Garaizar, J. (2006). Kefir: a symbiotic yeasts-bacteria community with alleged healthy capabilities. Rev Iberoam Micol, 23(2), 67-74.

33 Vujičić, I. F., Vulić, M., & Könyves, T. (1992). Assimilation of cholesterol in milk by kefir cultures. Biotechnology Letters, 14(9), 847-850.

34 Farnworth, E. R. (2006). Kefir–a complex probiotic. Food Science and Technology Bulletin: Fu, 2(1), 1-17.

35 Prado, M. R., Blandón, L. M., Vandenberghe, L. P., Rodrigues, C., Castro, G. R., Thomaz-Soccol, V., & Soccol, C. R. (2015). Milk kefir: composition, microbial cultures, biological activities, and related products. Frontiers in microbiology, 6.

36 Garrote, G. L., Abraham, A. G., & De Antoni, G. L. (1997). Preservation of kefir grains, a comparative study. LWT-food science and technology, 30(1), 77-84.

37 Farnworth, E. R. (2006). Kefir–a complex probiotic. Food Science and Technology Bulletin: Fu, 2(1), 1-17

38 Koroleva, M. S. (1991). Products prepared with lactic acid bacteria and yeasts. ELSEVIER APPL. FOOD SCI. SER., 159-179.

39 132. Maccaferri, S., Klinder, A., Brigidi, P., Cavina, P., & Costabile, A. (2012). Potential probiotic Kluyveromyces marxianus B0399 modulates the immune response in Caco-2 cells and peripheral blood mononuclear cells and impacts the human gut microbiota in an in vitro colonic model system. Applied and environmental microbiology, 78(4), 956-964.

133. Bourrie, B. C., Willing, B. P., & Cotter, P. D. (2016). The microbiota and health promoting characteristics of the fermented beverage kefir. Frontiers in microbiology, 7

40 Leite, A. M. D. O., Miguel, M. A. L., Peixoto, R. S., Rosado, A. S., Silva, J. T., & Paschoalin, V. M. F. (2013). Microbiological, technological and therapeutic properties of kefir: a natural probiotic beverage. Brazilian Journal of Microbiology, 44(2), 341-349.

41 Maeda, H., Zhu, X., Suzuki, S., Suzuki, K., & Kitamura, S. (2004). Structural characterization and biological activities of an exopolysaccharide kefiran produced by Lactobacillus kefiranofaciens WT-2BT. Journal of agricultural and food chemistry, 52(17), 5533-5538.

42 Liu, J. R., Wang, S. Y., Lin, Y. Y., & Lin, C. W. (2002). Antitumor activity of milk kefir and soy milk kefir in tumor-bearing mice. Nutrition and cancer, 44(2), 183-187.

43 Farnworth, E. R. (2006). Kefir–a complex probiotic. Food Science and Technology Bulletin: Fu, 2(1), 1-17

44 Farnworth, E. R. (2006). Kefir–a complex probiotic. Food Science and Technology Bulletin: Fu, 2(1), 1-17.

45 Liu, J. R., & Lin, C. W. (2000). Production of kefir from soymilk with or without added glucose, lactose, or sucrose. Journal of Food Science, 65(4), 716-719.

Gulitz, A., Stadie, J., Wenning, M., Ehrmann, M. A., & Vogel, R. F. (2011). The microbial diversity of water kefir. International journal of food microbiology, 151(3), 284-288.

46 Liu, J. R., Chen, M. J., & Lin, C. W. (2002). Characterization of polysaccharide and volatile compounds produced by kefir grains grown in soymilk. Journal of food science, 67(1), 104-108.

47 Bolla, P. A., Carasi, P., de los Angeles Bolla, M., De Antoni, G. L., & de los Angeles Serradell, M. (2013). Protective effect of a mixture of kefir-isolated lactic acid bacteria and yeasts in a hamster model of Clostridium difficile infection. Anaerobe, 21, 28-33

48 Farnworth, E. R. (2006). Kefir–a complex probiotic. Food Science and Technology Bulletin: Fu, 2(1), 1-17.

49 Bolla, P. A., Carasi, P., de los Angeles Bolla, M., De Antoni, G. L., & de los Angeles Serradell, M. (2013). Protective effect of a mixture of kefir-isolated lactic acid bacteria and yeasts in a hamster model of Clostridium difficile infection. Anaerobe, 21, 28-33.

50 Farnworth ER, Mainville I (2008) Kefir -A Fermented Milk Product. In: Farnworth, E. R. (2th ed.), Handbook of Fermented Functional Foods (2 ed). CRC Press Taylor & Francis Group, Boca Raton, London, New York, p. 89-127

51 Sachdeva, A., & Nagpal, J. (2009). Effect of fermented milk-based probiotic preparations on Helicobacter pylori eradication: a systematic review and meta-analysis of randomized-controlled trials. European journal of gastroenterology & hepatology, 21(1), 45-53.

52 Thoreux, K., & Schmucker, D. L. (2001). Kefir milk enhances intestinal immunity in young but not old rats. The Journal of nutrition, 131(3), 807-812.

53 Medrano, M., Racedo, S. M., Rolny, I. S., Abraham, A. G., & Pérez, P. F. (2011). Oral administration of kefiran induces changes in the balance of immune cells in a murine model. Journal of agricultural and food chemistry, 59(10), 5299-5304.

Vinderola, G., Perdigón, G., Duarte, J., Farnworth, E., & Matar, C. (2006). Effects of the oral administration of the exopolysaccharide produced by Lactobacillus kefiranofaciens on the gut mucosal immunity. Cytokine, 36(5), 254-260.

54 Farnworth, E. R. (2006). Kefir–a complex probiotic. Food

Science and Technology Bulletin: Fu, 2(1), 1-17.

55 Sakaguchi, S. (2011). Regulatory T cells: history and perspective. Regulatory T cells: methods and protocols, 3-17.

56 Carasi, P., Racedo, S. M., Jacquot, C., Romanin, D. E., Serradell, M. A., & Urdaci, M. C. (2015). Impact of kefir derived Lactobacillus kefiri on the mucosal immune response and gut microbiota. Journal of immunology research, 2015.

57 Sicherer, S. H., & Sampson, H. A. (2014). Food allergy: epidemiology, pathogenesis, diagnosis, and treatment. Journal of Allergy and Clinical Immunology, 133(2), 291-307.

58 Sjögren, Y. M., Jenmalm, M. C., Böttcher, M. F., Björkstén, B., & Sverremark-Ekström, E. (2009). Altered early infant gut microbiota in children developing allergy up to 5 years of age. Clinical & Experimental Allergy, 39(4), 518-526.

59 Hamet, M. F., Medrano, M., Perez, P. F., & Abraham, A. G. (2016). Oral administration of kefiran exerts a bifidogenic effect on BALB/c mice intestinal microbiota. Beneficial microbes, 7(2), 237-246.

Liu, J. R., Wang, S. Y., Chen, M. J., Chen, H. L., Yueh, P. Y., & Lin, C. W. (2006). Hypocholesterolaemic effects of milk-kefir and soyamilk-kefir in cholesterol-fed hamsters. British journal of nutrition, 95(5), 939-946.

60 Lee, M. Y., Ahn, K. S., Kwon, O. K., Kim, M. J., Kim, M. K., Lee, I. Y., ... & Lee, H. K. (2007). Anti-inflammatory and anti-allergic effects of kefir in a mouse asthma model. Immunobiology, 212(8), 647-654.

61 Huseini, H. F., Rahimzadeh, G., Fazeli, M. R., Mehrazma, M., & Salehi, M. (2012). Evaluation of wound healing activities of kefir products. Burns, 38(5), 719-723.

62 Tu, M. Y., Chen, H. L., Tung, Y. T., Kao, C. C., Hu, F. C., & Chen, C. M. (2015). Short-term effects of kefir-fermented milk consumption on bone mineral density and bone metabolism in a randomized clinical trial of osteoporotic patients. PloS one, 10(12), e0144231.

63 Wang, Y., Xu, N., Xi, A., Ahmed, Z., Zhang, B., & Bai, X. (2009). Effects of Lactobacillus plantarum MA2 isolated from Tibet kefir on lipid metabolism and intestinal microflora of rats fed on high-cholesterol diet. Applied microbiology and biotechnology, 84(2), 341-347.

Huang, Y., Wang, X., Wang, J., Wu, F., Sui, Y., Yang, L., & Wang, Z. (2013). Lactobacillus plantarum strains as potential probiotic cultures with cholesterol-lowering activity. Journal of dairy science, 96(5), 2746-2753.

Zheng, Y., Lu, Y., Wang, J., Yang, L., Pan, C., & Huang, Y. (2013). Probiotic properties of Lactobacillus strains isolated from Tibetan kefir grains. PloS one, 8(7), e69868.

64 Maeda, H., Zhu, X., Suzuki, S., Suzuki, K., & Kitamura, S. (2004). Structural characterization and biological activities of an exopolysaccharide kefiran produced by Lactobacillus kefiranofaciens WT-2BT. Journal of agricultural and food chemistry, 52(17), 5533-5538.

65 Leite, A. M. D. O., Miguel, M. A. L., Peixoto, R. S., Rosado, A. S., Silva, J. T., & Paschoalin, V. M. F. (2013). Microbiological, technological and therapeutic properties of kefir: a natural probiotic beverage. Brazilian Journal of Microbiology, 44(2), 341-349.

66 Gao, J., Gu, F., Ruan, H., Chen, Q., He, J., & He, G. (2013). Induction of apoptosis of gastric cancer cells SGC7901 in vitro by a cell-free fraction of Tibetan kefir. International Dairy Journal, 30(1), 14-18.

Ghoneum, M., & Gimzewski, J. (2014). Apoptotic effect of a novel kefir product, PFT, on multidrug-resistant myeloid leukemia cells via a hole-piercing mechanism. International journal of oncology, 44(3), 830-837.

67 Ley, R. E., Bäckhed, F., Turnbaugh, P., Lozupone, C. A., Knight, R. D., & Gordon, J. I. (2005). Obesity alters gut microbial ecology. Proceedings of the National Academy of Sciences of the United States of America, 102(31), 11070-11075.

68 Ley, R. E., Turnbaugh, P. J., Klein, S., & Gordon, J. I. (2006). Microbial ecology: human gut microbes associated with obesity. Nature, 444(7122), 1022.

69 Bercik, P., Verdu, E. F., Foster, J. A., Macri, J., Potter, M., Huang, X., ... & Lu, J. (2010). Chronic gastrointestinal inflammation induces anxiety-like behavior and alters central nervous system biochemistry in mice. Gastroenterology, 139(6), 2102-2112.

70 O'Brien, K. V., Stewart, L. K., Forney, L. A., Aryana, K. J., Prinyawiwatkul, W., & Boeneke, C. A. (2015). The effects of postexercise consumption of a kefir beverage on performance and recovery during intensive endurance training. Journal of dairy science, 98(11), 7446-7449.

71 Parodi A, Paolino S, Greco A, et al. Small intestinal bacterial overgrowth in rosacea: clinical effectiveness of its eradication. Clin Gastroenterol Hepatol. 2008;6(7):759-64.

Muizzuddin N, Maher W, Sullivan M, Schnittger S, Mammone T. Physiological effect of a probiotic on skin. J Cosmet Sci. 2012;63(6):385-95.

Di marzio L, Cinque B, De simone C, Cifone MG. Effect of the lactic acid bacterium Streptococcus thermophilus on ceramide levels in human keratinocytes in vitro and stratum corneum in vivo. J Invest Dermatol. 1999;113(1):98-106

72 Parodi, A., Paolino, S., Greco, A., Drago, F., Mansi, C., Rebora, A., ... & Savarino, V. (2008). Small intestinal bacterial overgrowth in rosacea: clinical effectiveness of its eradication. Clinical Gastroenterology and Hepatology, 6(7), 759-764.

73 Reid, G., & Burton, J. (2002). Use of Lactobacillus to prevent infection by pathogenic bacteria. Microbes and infection, 4(3), 319-324.

74 Reid, G., Charbonneau, D., Erb, J., Kochanowski, B., Beuerman, D., Poehner, R., & Bruce, A. W. (2003). Oral use of Lactobacillus rhamnosus GR-1 and L. fermentum RC-14 significantly alters vaginal flora: randomized, placebo-controlled trial in 64 healthy women. FEMS Immunology & Medical Microbiology, 35(2), 131-134.

75 Rautava, S., Kainonen, E., Salminen, S., & Isolauri, E. (2012). Maternal probiotic supplementation during pregnancy and breast-feeding reduces the risk of eczema in the infant. Journal of Allergy and Clinical Immunology, 130(6), 1355-1360.

76 Prescott, S. L., Wickens, K., Westcott, L., Jung, W., Currie, H., Black, P. N., ... & Wu, L. (2008). Supplementation with Lactobacillus rhamnosus or Bifidobacterium lactis probiotics in pregnancy increases cord blood interferon-γ and breast milk transforming growth factor-β and immunoglobin A detection. Clinical & Experimental Allergy, 38(10), 1606-1614.

77 Lindsay, K. L., Walsh, C. A., Brennan, L., & McAuliffe, F. M. (2013). Probiotics in pregnancy and maternal outcomes: a systematic review. The Journal of Maternal-Fetal & Neonatal Medicine, 26(8), 772-778.

78 Abkhasians The Long-Living People of the Caucasus by Sula Benet 1974

79 http://www.nytimes.com/1998/03/14/world/lerik-journal-yogurt-caucasus-centenarians-never-eat-it.html

80 Bourrie, B. C., Willing, B. P., & Cotter, P. D. (2016). The microbiota and health promoting characteristics of the fermented beverage kefir. Frontiers in microbiology, 7.

81 Santos, A., San Mauro, M., Sanchez, A., Torres, J. M., & Marquina, D. (2003). The antimicrobial properties of different strains of Lactobacillus spp. isolated from kefir. Systematic and Applied Microbiology, 26(3), 434-437.

Printed in Great Britain
by Amazon